THE GOVERNMENT AND
POLITICS OF
THE SOVIET UNION

Leonard Schapiro

*Formerly Professor of Political Science, with special reference to
Russian Studies, in the University of London*

Hutchinson
London Melbourne Sydney Auckland Johannesburg

Hutchinson & Co. (Publishers) Ltd

An imprint of the Hutchinson Publishing Group

17-21 Conway Street, London W1P 6JD

Hutchinson Publishing Group (Australia) Pty Ltd
16-22 Church Street, Hawthorn, Melbourne, Victoria 3122

Hutchinson Group (NZ) Ltd
32-34 View Road, PO Box 40-086, Glenfield, Auckland 10

Hutchinson Group (SA) (Pty) Ltd
PO Box 337, Bergvlei 2012, South Africa

First published 1965
Second (revised) edition 1967
Third edition 1968
Fourth edition 1970
Fifth edition 1973
Reprinted 1975
Sixth edition 1977
Reprinted with revisions 1979
Reprinted 1982, 1984, 1985

© Leonard Schapiro 1965, 1967, 1968, 1970, 1973 and 1977

Printed and bound in Great Britain by
Anchor Brendon Ltd, Tiptree, Essex

British Library Cataloguing in Publication Data
Schapiro, Leonard
    The government and politics of the Soviet Union –
    6th ed.
    1. Soviet Union – Politics and government – 19th
    century   2. Soviet Union – Politics and
    government – 20th century
    I. Title
    320.947   JN6511

        ISBN 0 09 131721 5 paper

CONTENTS

NOTE TO THE SIXTH EDITION

The information for this edition has been brought up to date by the insertion of the latest facts available in January 1977. I have also added a new chapter summarising the main political developments of the past ten years. I am much indebted to Miss Xenia Howard-Johnston for her help.

NOTE TO THE SECOND EDITION (1967)

Since this book appeared important changes have taken place in the government of the Soviet Union and a number of changes made during the time when N. S. Khrushchev was First Secretary of the CPSU have been repealed. In the first edition which was completed for the press around the time of Khrushchev's fall only very hasty alterations were possible. This second edition has been completely revised so as to take account of changes up to June 1966 so far as they are known. I have also followed the advice of some reviewers and brought the historical chapter up to date from the death of Stalin, where I had left it in the first edition.

I am once again deeply indebted to my colleague Paul Rosta for his skill and patience in helping me with the revision of this book, for checking factual information. and for once again preparing the Index.

L.S.

ACKNOWLEDGMENTS IN THE FIRST EDITION (1965)

My thanks are due to Professor W. A. Robson, the general editor of this series, for his warm encouragement and friendly help and advice. I am also most grateful to Dr I. Lapenna, Dr S. V. Utechin and Mr H. T. Willetts for their kindness and patience in reading the manuscript and saving me from innumerable errors. The errors which remain are my own. My thanks are also due to Mrs M. Thomas for her skill in preparing the manuscript and, as always, to my wife for critical help at all stages. I owe a special debt of gratitude to Mr Paul Rosta, who checked the whole work, suggested numerous corrections and improvements and prepared the Index.

L.S.

SOME COMMONLY USED RUSSIAN TERMS

AND ABBREVIATIONS

ASSR	Autonomous Soviet Socialist Republic
CC (or TsK)	Central Committee
Cheka	A local commission of Vecheka, but often used for Vecheka
CPSU	Communist Party of the Soviet Union
Gorispolkom	City (Soviet) Executive Committee
Gorkom	City (party) Committee
Gosarbitrazh	State Arbitration
Gosbank	State Bank
Gosplan	State Planning Committee
Gosstroi	State Construction Committee
GPU	State Political Directorate
Ispolkom	Executive Committee
KGB	Committee for State Security
Kolkhoz	Collective Farm
Komsomol	All-Union Leninist Communist League of Youth
Krai	Area
Kraikom	Area (party) Committee
MGB	Ministry for State Security
MVD	Ministry for Internal Affairs
NEP	New Economic Policy
NKGB	People's Commissariat for State Security
NKVD	People's Commissariat for Internal Affairs
Obkom	Regional (party) Committee

Oblast	Region
Oblispolkom	Regional (Soviet) Executive Committee
OGPU	United State Political Directorate
Okrug	Circuit
Raiispolkom	District (Soviet) Executive Committee
Raikom	District (party) Committee
Raion	District
RSFSR	Russian Soviet Federal Socialist Republic
Selsoviet	Rural Soviet
Sovkhoz	State Farm
Soviet	Council
Sovnarkhoz	Council of National Economy
USSR	Union of Soviet Socialist Republics
Vecheka	All-Russian Extraordinary Commission for Combating Counter-Revolution, Sabotage and Speculation
Vesenkha	Supreme Council of National Economy (SCNE)

INTRODUCTION

Many pitfalls await the student of Soviet government. Not least is the problem of sources. For one thing, there are no Soviet textbooks of government such as we know in our own political literature—only textbooks of constitutional and public law. It is as if, for example, the literature on British government were confined to the textbooks of constitutional law alone: if we had nothing else to read or to learn from we should emerge with the conviction—to choose one among many—that the Queen in Parliament is the sovereign power in England; we should know little of parties, of the predominance of the Cabinet, of the role of the civil service or of pressure groups. Fortunately we have a wealth of other material to draw on: memoirs, spirited and controversial debate both in parliament and in the press, and a great deal of opportunity for personal contact with and experience of the business of government.

Very little of all this exists in the case of the Soviet Union, at any rate for the foreign student. There are virtually no memoirs of recent events, public debate is nearly always very formal, the press is strictly controlled and the foreigner at all events has few chances for personal investigation of and contact with government in action. Yet this is not to say that academic study of Soviet government must be given up in despair—a considerable body of scholarly literature in English on both sides of the Atlantic and the experience of teaching in our universities provide a powerful argument to the contrary. The study may be harder than, say, that of Switzerland or Sweden. But the academic method is the

same: to seek out the true nature and function of institutions, to
determine the real seat of power, to discern trends of evolution.
And in all this to be swayed neither by a political bias which
accepts uncritically all the lofty claims which the Soviet leaders
make for their own form of government; nor yet to allow prejudice
of any kind to search out defects where they do not exist; to be
understanding of problems and to be slow to condemn.

For such a study there is evidence enough for those who are
diligent in the search. Even a controlled press and formal debate
can be very revealing of conflicts under the surface. History is a
powerful aid: with fifty-one years of experience to draw on, even
the most disciplined public debates can be seen to reflect the
realities of politics behind the façade of unanimity. Changes in the
law and changes of appointments tell their story in the Soviet
Union as in any other political system.

Sources apart, there are, in my experience, three aspects of the
study of Soviet government which must always be borne in mind.
First, the confusion of nomenclature. Although Soviet government is government of a novel type, it follows the disconcerting
practice of using traditional terms for institutions which bear little
or no relationship to the prototypes whose names they have
borrowed. Take 'Communist Party'. Traditionally and etymo-
logically a 'party' is one of several groups contending for a share
of power in the state. In Soviet usage the term is applied to one
group which, so far from contending for power, exercises a virtual
monopoly of power and is, as will be seen, doctrinally considered
to be entitled to this monopoly. Or again, 'election'; this term
means to choose, 'to choose in preference to an alternative',
according to the *Shorter Oxford English Dictionary*. The Soviet
voter has no alternative, and his ballot for the single candidate,
while it may be a political act of some value, is obviously not
'election' in its ordinary meaning. These instances could be
multiplied.

Next, there is the importance of theory. The USSR is a revolutionary society. It came into being for the avowed purpose of
putting into effect the theories about society of Marx and Engels,
as developed by Lenin. Its institutions show the influence of those
theories at every point. There are some who take the view that too
much importance should not be attached to theory. They would
argue that, however important it may have been in bringing about
the Bolshevik revolution and the early stages of Soviet develop-

ment, the main problems now are problems of power, as in any other state. I think there is some truth in this view, particularly in the sense that questions of theory are often seen in practice to become subordinated to issues of power, to be used as instruments, as it were, for the assertion or maintenance of power. Nevertheless, to ignore theory is to see only half the picture. To choose only one example: the very legitimacy of the Communist Party, the basis of its claim to wield the power that it does, is founded squarely on Lenin's theory; if you take away that theory, that article of faith, the whole legitimacy of the revolution is put at issue, and with it the legitimacy of the heirs of the revolution, the present rulers of the USSR.

Finally, there is the importance of history. This is not peculiar to the case of the USSR: no system of government can be understood without some knowledge of its evolution and of the roots from which it derives. The circumstances in which Lenin's party, the Bolsheviks, became the dominant party have left their indelible mark. The nature of the revolutions of 1917 (there were two) shaped the future of the Soviet state. The pattern of Stalin's 'third revolution'—rapid industrialisation, collectivisation of agriculture and total control over society—determines the shape of government today. It is to history therefore that we turn at the outset.

I

THE ORIGINS OF BOLSHEVISM

It is customary to date the origin of the Russian Social Democratic movement, the ancestor of the ultimately victorious Bolsheviks, from the First Congress of the All-Russian Social Democratic Labour Party, which met in Minsk in March 1898. In fact, this Congress was hardly representative and of little practical influence. The history of Bolshevism must be looked for both earlier and later.

The doctrines of Marx were known and studied in Russia as early as the 1860's, if not before. (The first volume of *Capital* was openly published in Russian translation in 1872—the censorship regarded it as too academic and irrelevant to Russian conditions to be subversive.) Until the last decade of the century Russia remained a largely agricultural country with little industry and a small industrial proletariat. Marx's general prophecy of a necessary historical evolution from a system of private capitalism to a system of socialism, in which the overwhelming majority of the population, the proletariat, would become the dominant class, meant little in Russia where capitalism in the western, industrial sense was undeveloped. Indeed, until the eighties, the predominant doctrine, the doctrine of the Populists (*Narodniki*), held that Russia could and should avoid the capitalist path of development by pursuing a path of her own. Central to the Populist faith was the conviction that the traditional village peasant commune would provide a nucleus and a model for the future social order, which would be superior to the capitalist order. Marx never committed himself to the view that his doctrines were relevant to Russia and indeed on one occasion protested against the attempts of the Russian Populist Mikhailovsky 'to transform my sketch of the origins of capitalism in western Europe into a historical philosophical theory of a universal movement necessarily imposed upon all peoples. . . .'

This was written in 1877. Yet not long after Marx's death in 1883 this was precisely what the leading Russian exponents of Marxism were engaged in doing. For changes were becoming discernible on the Russian scene which made Marx's analysis appear more relevant, at any rate to some thinkers. In 1883 Georgiy Plekhanov (1857–1918), who had left Russia a few years before, founded in Geneva the Liberation of Labour Group, together with Paul Akselrod (1850–1928), Lev Deich (1855–1941) and Vera Zasulich (1851–1919). It was a theoretical Marxist group with a very practical aim: to publish Marxist literature for dissemination inside Russia, and to help to create inside Russia a Social Democratic party which would be ready, when the time came, to lead the forthcoming revolution. In a series of pamphlets, which found their way, as intended, into Russia, Plekhanov argued that the village commune on which the Populists pinned their faith was already fast disintegrating; that Russia had already entered on to the path of capitalist development, and must therefore inevitably follow the same course of progress—first towards a bourgeois democratic revolution in which the autocracy would be replaced by a regime of democratic freedom; and thereafter in the fullness of time towards the final proletarian socialist revolution. His arguments could, by 1890, be supported by the visible growth of an industrial proletariat, which was beginning to express discontent with its often abjectly miserable conditions in strikes and demonstrations; and by the undoubted signs of the beginnings of industrial 'take-off'.

Inside Russia too, under the influence both of Plekhanov and of the German Social Democratic theorists, leading Marxists were emerging into public debate, conducted within the limits of a growingly suspicious censorship. Among these advocates of Marxism against the hitherto dominant Populists were three outstanding writers whose future careers were to follow very different lines: Vladimir Ilyich Ulianov, better known by his adopted name of Lenin (1870–1924), who was to become the leader of the Bolsheviks; A. N. Potresov (1869–1934), one of the leaders of the Mensheviks; and P. B. Struve (1870–1944), who by the end of the century forsook Marxism and became one of the leaders of the liberal movement. These divergences were symptomatic of two characteristics of early Russian Marxist theory. First, of the way in which Marxism, as a pattern of modernisation and westernisation for a relatively backward and autocratic society, appealed to men of very different temperaments; and secondly, of the fact that it was primarily as a result of the form of revolutionary activity which each of these leaders adopted that his future belief and principles were shaped.

It is now necessary to turn from this realm of almost academic theory to the background of revolutionary activity inside Russia upon which the theory was soon to be grafted. Revolutionary action, largely dominated by the Populist philosophy of A. I. Herzen (1812–1870) and the wilder anarchism of M. Bakunin (1814–1876), began, in the main, after the emancipation of the serfs in 1861. Its centre of attention was the peasantry, its lodestar and hope the village commune. Although it did not lack its more violent elements, especially among the followers of Bakunin, the advocate of destruction as a creative force, its ambitions were social, not political. The aim was an ultimate peasant revolution, and most of the revolutionaries saw their main task not as a conspiracy, so much as an attempt by propaganda among the peasants to train the leaders of the future. They were for the most part romantic, naive, idealistic and in Russian conditions doomed to repeated failures and disappointment. But there were exceptions. One such, whose writings may have considerably influenced the young Lenin, among others, was P. N. Tkachev (1844–1885). Tkachev, from his exile in Switzerland, urged the need for a conspiracy by an élite to seize power at the top. He argued that the opportunity was running out, because, when once capitalism developed, the autocracy, at present (the beginning of the seventies) without support, would have powerful interests to lean on. Thought of social revolution by the peasants was an illusion: it was essential to seize power first, and then to effect social reforms from above.

Less as a result of Tkachev's influence than as a consequence of progressive disillusionment, the Populist revolutionaries did in fact generate a party of conspiracy. In 1879 their party, known as *Land and Liberty*, was split in two: one section, which took the name of *The People's Will*, declared war on the autocracy, and their activity culminated in the assassination of Alexander II on

1 March 1881. Among those who broke with his associates on this issue of their change from the 'social' to the 'political' revolution was Plekhanov, who by 1881 was already on the way to becoming a convert to Marxism.

The assassination of the Emperor, incidentally the most moderate autocrat who ever ruled over Russia, accomplished nothing. The reaction which set in succeeded by fresh repressions in breaking *The People's Will*, though isolated conspiracies and assassinations continued. One such conspiracy, to assassinate the Emperor, was discovered in 1887. Lenin's elder brother, Alexander Ulianov, was hanged for his part in it—an incident which must rightly be regarded as one of the most formative in the future leader's life. The débâcle of Populism gave impetus to the Marxist revolutionary movement. In the eighties, and especially in the nineties, underground groups and circles were springing up all over Russia among the growing working class. These groups were led by Marxist intellectuals or in some cases by educated workers and out of these the future Social Democratic party was to grow. It is important to realise, in the light of subsequent developments, the temper and motives at this time of the majority of these Marxists. They found in Marxism a promise of an inexorable social trend, which with historic inevitability would lead Russia to an essentially social revolution, through the path of capitalism. Their Marxism was thus at the same time a hope of westernisation and industrialisation for Russia, the road to democratic freedoms and a revulsion against the voluntarist form which Populism in its last phase had adopted. Plekhanov was one of the influences on their thought and he while urging the need for a Social Democratic party which would take the lead in the forthcoming revolutions—both the democratic and the ultimate social revolutions—was a violent opponent of the conspiratorial, Jacobin revolutionaries. Like Engels before him, he had crossed swords at an early stage with Tkachev. But Plekhanov was an *émigré* and a theorist. The dominant influence inside Russia was the practical experience of leading the growing worker movement of protest, with its inevitably greater emphasis on practical objectives than on ultimate political aims. Here was a future source of disagreement; and indeed by the end of the century Plekhanov came into sharp collision with the new leaders from inside Russia when some of them appeared in Switzerland.

Lenin's apprenticeship as a revolutionary was served after 1887, first in Kazan and then in Samara. His conversion to Marxism, though not his first acquaintance with it, took place (according to his own account fifteen years later) in the beginning of 1889. Lenin was thus a revolutionary before he became a Marxist, and in his early years appears to have been exposed to influences of some of the Populist revolutionaries who belonged to the Jacobin tradition. But having embraced Marxism he threw himself into the study and propagation of it among his revolutionary colleagues with the energy and force of persuasion which always characterised him. In 1893 he moved to St Petersburg, the capital, to continue his work in the Marxist underground. He also visited Plekhanov and the other leaders of Russian Social Democracy in Switzerland. In 1895, together with the future leader of Menshevism, Julius Martov (Tsederbaum, 1873–1923), he formed the Petersburg Union of Struggle for the Liberation of the Working Class, to disseminate Marxist ideas in worker circles and to prepare the leaders of the future revolution. His connection with the Union was shortlived for he was soon arrested and spent the next four and a half years first in prison, and then in Siberian exile. The conditions of his exile were comfortable and he was able to obtain materials to prepare his influential work, *The Development of Capitalism in Russia*, published legally in 1899. This book was directed against the Populist theorists and argued, on the basis of a wealth of statistical material, the inevitable onset, and indeed the existence already, in Russia of capitalism on the western European model—the necessary precondition for the rest of the deductions on social development drawn by Marx in respect of the industrial countries of western Europe and the United States. A powerful contribution to the debate against the Populists had already been made by Struve in 1894, with the publication of his *Critical Remarks on the Question of the Economic Development of Russia*. But whereas Struve had been more concerned to argue that the advent of capitalism should be welcomed, since it would, along with its miseries, bring the material and spiritual culture of western Europe, including political liberty, to Russia, Lenin was more concerned to show that capitalism in Russia was already an accomplished fact, and that it contained all the conditions for economic viability.

Meanwhile underground Marxism as a political movement was growing fast in Russia towards the close of the century. There were Marxist circles and committees in all the main industrial

towns and districts of the Russian Empire, and strike activity was
on the increase. Considerable impetus to the whole movement was
given by the influence of the Social Democratic organisations of
the Jewish pale, which in 1897 united into the *General Jewish
Workers' Union in Lithuania, Poland and Russia*, known as the
Bund. It was through the influence of the Jewish Social Democratic organisations in 1895, in the first instance through the agency
of Martov, that the whole of the Russian movement was reshaped.
Hitherto it had tended to be confined to small conspiratorial
circles of future revolutionary leaders, for the most part intellectuals in origin. Now the attempt was made to enlist wider support
among workers and to spread Marxist ideas in simpler form but
to a wider extent. The practical consequences of this development,
which took place mainly while Lenin and Martov were imprisoned
or in exile, were twofold. In the first place the effect of this expansion of the movement was to increase the risk of discovery and of
governmental repression and to create the strong sense of the need
for conspiratorial action which was to dominate much of the
theory of Russian Social Democracy among many of its leaders
thereafter. Secondly, the aim to attract a wider mass following
dictated, so far as the leaders were concerned, a need to concen-
trate on practical objectives such as better wages and working
conditions, which were capable of achievement by strikes. Revolutionary slogans, directed towards the overthrow of the autocracy, tended to frighten and repel the workers. It was the doctrine
of the leaders of the movement inside Russia, which was in fact
largely borne out by events, that in Russian conditions the workers
would soon learn in practice that the struggle for 'economic'
objectives led inevitably and inexorably to the demand for
'political' objectives. They believed that it would be better for the
worker Social Democrats to learn this lesson in practice than to
have it forced upon them through exhortation by their leaders.

This view was not shared by Plekhanov and his fellow ideolo-
gists in Switzerland, who, out of touch perhaps with Russian conditions, argued dogmatically for the primacy of political objectives. They had, however, done little to resolve the first difficulty
which beset any attempt to apply Marxism as a practical doctrine
of action to Russian conditions. For Marxism presupposed a long
process before the proletarian revolution could be accomplished.
In the first place, the 'feudal' autocracy must give way to the rule
of the bourgeoisie, in a 'bourgeois' or 'democratic' revolution.

This would open up to the proletariat opportunities for organising and developing its movement. In the fullness of time the proletariat, having become the overwhelming majority in a fully developed capitalist society, would effect the 'proletarian' or 'socialist' revolution. It is indeed obvious that such a doctrine required of its followers, in a still largely peasant country at the end of the last century, a more considerable degree of patience than can be expected of revolutionaries. The only practical contribution (mainly by Akselrod) to this problem of impatience was provided by the theory of 'hegemony'. According to this, the working class, as the most consciously advanced class in Russia, was to exercise 'hegemony' over the middle-class parties when the time came for them to effect the democratic revolution, so as to ensure that they did not fail for lack of resolution. There were no middle-class parties in Russia in 1899 but experience was to show when they made their appearance a few years later that the doctrine of 'hegemony' was largely meaningless in practice. It was Lenin who was to provide a more effective short-cut to revolution. It is a matter of controversy how much of the previous conceptions of Marxism as a social process was preserved in the result.

Plekhanov's conflict with the leaders of the movement inside Russia has already been referred to. This conflict was considerably exacerbated by the development in German Social Democracy, under the influence of Eduard Bernstein (1850–1932) of the movement known variously as 'reformism' or 'revisionism'. Bernstein's most influential pamphlet appeared in 1899, entitled (in its English translation which appeared in 1909) *Evolutionary Socialism*. Bernstein attacked the economic foundations of Marxism in the light of actual developments and argued that the policy of reforms brought about by strong pressures through democratic means had in fact achieved more for the workers than could ever be won by revolution. The real purpose of socialism could best be achieved when the socialist party worked jointly with the radical bourgeoisie for reform. A dictatorship of the proletariat could in practice only mean a dictatorship by a minority of revolutionary leaders.

This doctrine had a few intellectual followers in Russia, notably Struve, as long as he remained a Marxist, and E. D. Kuskova (1869–1959). It cannot fairly be said that it presented any intellectual appeal for the practical leaders of the Russian Social Democratic movement, who continued to support 'economic' action by the workers mainly as a natural step to 'political' action. However, Bernstein and his doctrine became the objects of spirited attack by Plekhanov and his followers, including Lenin, Martov and Potresov, when their exile ended by the beginning of 1900. The attack was not confined to theory: wrapped up with it was an attack on the leadership of the movement inside Russia, whose policy was branded as 'economism', meaning by this the denial of of the need for political action and reliance solely on pressure for economic reforms. This attack was the beginning of the process by which the Swiss exiles asserted their leadership over the movement in Russia.

In the course of his exile Lenin had evolved the idea of creating a newspaper printed outside Russia which would not only serve to safeguard the Russian Social Democratic movement from the ideological contamination of 'economism' but would also form an organisational centre for unifying the Russian underground committees. This scheme was put into effect when the first issue of the newspaper, *Iskra* ('Spark'), appeared in Leipzig on 24 December 1900. The editorial board consisted of Plekhanov (with two votes), Akselrod, Vera Zasulich, Potresov, Martov and Lenin. For the time being these very different leaders were united in the fight against 'economism'; at any rate no differences of opinion were allowed to emerge into the open. *Iskra*, as Lenin intended, was much more than a newspaper smuggled into Russia by secret couriers. It also organised a network of underground agents inside Russia whose task was to win over the underground committees to allegiance to *Iskra*. The methods employed by these agents in winning control over the committees in the face of the resistance of many of them to these self-nominated leaders abroad were often far from democratic. Usually their aim was to effect a split and then to use the pro-*Iskra* elements to secure domination over the whole committee. By the spring of 1903 the overwhelming majority of the committees had been won over by one means or another.

The time was now considered ripe for summoning a Congress of the party. Although the foundation First Congress had been held in 1898, the Second Congress, which met in Brussels (later transferred to London) in July 1903, was to prove the more influential. It was composed overwhelmingly of supporters of *Iskra* —*Iskra* could command at least forty-one out of the fifty-one votes. Had the apparent unity of the *Iskra* movement been real, a united party would have emerged from the Congress. But behind the façade of unity lay deep divisions, which had been shelved in the enthusiasm of the battle against the 'economists'. They now came to the fore and by the end of the Congress the party was openly split into two factions. Lenin's faction had a majority of five votes. They therefore called themselves the 'majoritarians', or Bolsheviks, and dubbed their opponents the 'minoritarians', or Mensheviks—the names remained in use for years thereafter even though the balance of support in the party for each faction had changed.

The reason for the split was only in part to be found in questions of doctrine. It is true that the first division on the votes came over the question of the definition of a party member: Lenin's stricter formulation limited party membership to those who personally participated in one of the party organisations; Martov's formula extended recognition of party membership to those who gave 'regular personal co-operation'. While these formulae (quite academic in Russian conditions at the time) may be said to reflect different approaches to party discipline, it is also important to recall that Lenin and Martov had had no disagreements hitherto on the subject (though it was often discussed) and that in general such hesitations as were felt about Lenin's views on the nature of the party to be created were left in abeyance by all his five colleagues on *Iskra*. It therefore seems more probable to suppose that the root of the trouble is to be sought in abortive efforts made behind the scenes by Lenin (before this crucial vote) to exclude Potresov, Vera Zasulich and Akselrod from the board of *Iskra*, which was still designed by him to remain the centre of control over the entire party.

Whatever the immediate cause of the split, later developments showed that there existed a basic disagreement between Lenin and, in different degrees, all five of his colleagues over the nature of the party to be created and the split into two factions was destined, in spite of repeated efforts at reunification up to 1917, to remain permanent. Lenin's former colleagues, and now his opponents, succeeded in retaining possession of *Iskra* and in its pages attacked Lenin's doctrine of party leadership which they had hitherto, outwardly at any rate, fully supported. Lenin, for a time in isolation, worked actively to rebuild an organisation loyal to his leadership and succeeded in founding a rival paper, *Vpered* ('Forward'). By 1905 he succeeded in calling a somewhat unrepresentative gathering of delegates of pro-Bolshevik committees, which described itself as a Congress. The Mensheviks also met separately in conference.

Meanwhile Russia was experiencing a revolutionary year. The first overt attacks on an outmoded, oppressive and unimaginative autocratic system came at the end of 1904 from those sections of society from which the future liberal parties were to evolve. These were the organs of local self-government, the *Zemstva*, first set up in 1864, and the professional classes. This was not strictly a bourgeoisie, which in Russia did not exist in the sense in which a commercial middle class existed in contemporary England, but more an amalgam of liberal landowners and of intellectuals. From the agitation of the liberals grew the general unrest in the country, where ample grounds for discontent existed in all classes. On 9/22 January 1905[1] (*Bloody Sunday*) the whole country was shocked when an improvised, unarmed popular demonstration was fired on with many casualties. Defeat in the war with Japan added to the general sense of inarticulate rebellion which characterised the whole revolutionary movement. Unrest grew throughout the year but it was of a very largely unorganised character. The liberal parties only came into existence towards the end of the year. The socialists, both the Social Democrats and the Socialist Revolution-aries (whose main supporters were the peasants), proved incapable of leading an effective revolution. Though their agitation added fuel to the fire and helped to stimulate the temper out of which grew strikes and peasant disturbances, they were in no sense at the head of the movement. The Social Democrats, both the Bolsheviks and the Mensheviks, were as yet a small network of underground committees with little mass organisation or indeed following—with the possible exception of the *Bund* in the areas of the Jewish pale, where something approximating to a mass party existed. For the rest of the year there was a complete deadlock. The middle classes were incapable of pushing unrest to complete victory, and the revolutionaries were unable, because in the last resort the troops remained loyal to the regime, to achieve much more than a few risings. Yet each gained something in the process.

For the Social Democrats the most significant achievement, at any rate for their future development, was the setting up of revo-lutionary Soviets or councils in the capital and in many other cities. These Soviets were mass workers' bodies, which appear to have grown out of strike committees, but in the short time of their

1. Superior figures refer to notes at end of chapters.

existence exerted quite considerable influence on the turbulent events. They were mostly non-party in composition, though led by Social Democrats and Socialist Revolutionaries (the agrarian party, descended from the Populists). In the main the Mensheviks predominated in them, and indeed Lenin seems to have regarded the Petersburg Soviet with a certain amount of suspicion as a body which was likely to exhibit that unorganised 'spontaneity' in action which he always deplored. The most famous of these Soviets, the Petersburg Soviet, where L. Trotsky (1879–1940) first made his name, was short-lived and did not in the end achieve very much. But it set its mark on the future and, as will be seen, in a considerably transmuted form became the symbol of revolutionary power in 1917.

The more lasting achievement was the exaction from the Emperor on 17/30 October of a manifesto which promised full civil freedom and a State Duma, or legislature, to be elected on wide suffrage with full legislative powers. Even in the modified form in which the Fundamental Laws were enacted, they were a momentous change, since they transformed the autocracy into a constitutional monarchy—at any rate on paper. For the Social Democrats it raised the practical problems of their policy towards the future Duma, and of their relations with the two main liberal or centre parties, which now came into being—the Constitutional Democrats and the Octobrists.

In the heat of battle during 1905 the two factions of the Social Democrats had drawn closer together so far as the rank and file were concerned. The leaders remained divided on the issues which Lenin had precipitated in 1903 and on which he remained unyielding. But Bolsheviks and Mensheviks alike had strained their utmost together to bring about a national rising—both factions had taken part in the short abortive rising in Moscow at the end of 1905, the defeat of which by the government had at last broken the back of the revolutionary year. There was a spontaneous movement for reunification among the rank and file, which the leaders could not resist, and at a Congress in Stockholm in 1906 the party was nominally reunited. How far there was any intention on the Bolshevik side to make the reunification a reality may be doubted. At any rate, the 'shot-gun marriage', as Lenin's close associate, G. Zinoviev (1883–1936), was later to describe it, was not destined to last long. Meanwhile, Lenin maintained, at first clandestinely and then openly, a Bolshevik 'centre' separately organised as a rival to the Bolshevik/Menshevik Central Committee elected by the Congress.

From 1906 until 1912, when the Bolsheviks formally set themselves up as a separate party, relations between the two factions or parties remained very strained. There were three reasons for this. Although these differed in their nature, behind them lay a fundamental difference of view on the way to make a revolution. On the Bolshevik side—the conviction that the most important element was leadership and the determination of the most energetic Bolshevik, Lenin, that his own organisation must be preserved in disciplined and 'monolithic' form whatever the immediate consequences. On the Menshevik side—a growing belief that the revolution could be accomplished by the workers 'as a class', who would be trained and hardened in the kind of action in the defence of their rights that became possible within the circumscribed constitutional structure which existed in Russia after 1906. This said, it is necessary to add that this rather formal division was much complicated by the existence of various shades of opinion within each faction, which helped to foster the illusion that unity of the whole movement could still be achieved. On the other hand what divided Bolsheviks and Mensheviks in the last resort was temperament and the breach between them was constantly widened by personal animosities and intrigue.

Of the three issues which divided the two wings of the movement after 1906 the first in point of chronology was the matter of party funds. The Bolsheviks, less scrupulous or more determined than their rivals, succeeded in keeping possession for the use of their own organisation of large sums of money of doubtful origin—one such sum certainly came from armed hold-ups, another fortune from a bequest which the Mensheviks always considered had been left to the party as a whole and not to the one faction. The possession of these sums gave the Bolsheviks an advantage over their rivals in the matter of clandestine organisation of the underground committees which they soon learned to exploit. But it was also the subject of heated and acrimonious dispute which went a long way to wreck whatever slender chances there were of unity.

The next matter in dispute arose over working-class activities within the limits permitted after 1906—trade unions, mass conferences, the legal press and, above all, activity in the Duma, which came into existence in 1906. The Mensheviks, and more particularly those who remained active inside Russia, saw in these opportunities (frustrated as they frequently were by the arbitrary power which the Russian executive still retained, in spite of the promises of the October Manifesto,) some chance to create the kind of party of conscious workers which they understood the movement described by Marx to be. Partly as the result of Bolshevik financial and political operations, they conceived a disgust for the clandestine party organisations which were being constantly disrupted by intrigue. The Bolsheviks retaliated by accusing the Mensheviks of seeking to 'liquidate' the underground party—an accusation which, so far as the great majority of them were concerned, was not true. But it was an effective political argument—and became even more effective when Plekhanov, who had since 1903 remained mostly on the Menshevik side, quarrelled with his Menshevik colleagues in 1909 and began to side with Lenin (without joining the Bolshevik faction) in his campaign against the 'liquidators'.

The third issue between the two parties was the attitude to the Duma. The Mensheviks grew in time to treat the Duma as a serious forum for political action: this view was often shared by Bolshevik members too, but was rejected by Lenin, for whom the Duma was merely a sham to be exposed, though a valuable forum for unrestricted propaganda. In spite of Lenin's efforts, the small (Bolshevik and Menshevik) Social Democratic group in the Duma (there were only thirteen in the fourth Duma elected in 1912) remained more or less united—indeed, the worker electors whom they represented insisted on unity. It was therefore a considerable shock, not only for the Russian movement but for Social Democratic parties outside, when in October 1913 Lenin, after long efforts, succeeded in splitting the Duma Social Democrats into two hostile parties. Bolshevism now probably reached its lowest ebb.

The Second International took a hand in condemning Bolshevik tactics, and but for the First World War Lenin might well have found himself isolated from the entire Social Democratic movement. But the outbreak of war put an end to the intervention of the International in Russian Social Democracy and created a new situation for both the Bolsheviks and the Mensheviks.

On the outbreak of war the Russian Social Democratic groups, or 'fractions' in the Duma, both Bolshevik and Menshevik, voted against war credits. The Russians were the only Social Democrats, apart from the Serbians, to take this stand on the war: all other parties in the belligerent countries went back on their promises to oppose the war made in the Second International in 1907 and 1910 and sided with their governments when war broke out. But the Russian movement as a whole remained disunited. The Bolsheviks in the main were the most radical opponents of war. The Mensheviks also for the most part opposed it, though one wing of the party—including both Plekhanov and his small group and the 'practicals' or so-called 'liquidators'—supported the war effort: they believed that the Central Powers must at all costs be defeated and that socialist demands must be postponed until after victory.

Common opposition to the war had the natural tendency to draw Bolsheviks and Mensheviks closer together than they had been for many years. But there were also two factors which accentuated disunity. In the first place Lenin and his close followers went so far as to advocate the defeat of Russia as the 'lesser evil', and urged socialists in the belligerent countries to turn the war into a civil war: the Mensheviks, for the most part, limited themselves to calling for a just peace, to opposing territorial war aims and to advocating disarmament and co-operation for peace after hostilities had ended. Secondly, Lenin's final breach with all Social Democrats was sealed by his proclaimed intention to further the creation of a Third Communist International.

At this point it is convenient to consider the doctrine which has become known as 'Leninism' or 'Marxism-Leninism'. For it was this doctrine which was to influence the form of rule after October 1917 when the Bolshevik party established itself in power in Russia.

Lenin's ideas were only in part formed by 1903 and his system as a whole has to be studied over the years as it evolved in the heat of experience. Nor is there any complete, concrete system always to be discerned. There are, however, three vital topics on which his views were fairly clearly formulated between 1902 and 1917, namely—the role and nature of the party; the nature of the forthcoming revolution; and the nature of the state.

The role of the party, Lenin's most original contribution to Marxism or transformation of Marxism—according to one's views—is contained in *What is To Be Done?*, a pamphlet written in the autumn of 1901 and published in the spring of the following year. It was primarily an attack on 'economism' and a justification for the leading role claimed by *Iskra*. It is probably Lenin's

most significant work, though its significance only became fully
apparent when its key idea was put into practice—indeed at the
time, Plekhanov, Akselrod and Potresov, inspite of private mis-
givings, welcomed *What is To Be Done?* for its vigorous polemics.
The dominant argument is that 'the history of all countries proves'
that workers are of their own accord capable only of developing
a 'trade union consciousness'—the conviction that they must unite
for the struggle against their employers in order to improve their
material conditions. The ideas of 'scientific socialism', which
postulate the need for the social revolution, can only be brought
to the workers by intellectuals 'from the outside'; and the workers
must be led by professional full-time revolutionaries. The function
of these professional leaders of the vanguard of the working class
is to lead it, by means of effective organisation, to make the social
revolution which it is not capable of making itself—'Give us an
organisation of revolutionaries and we will overturn the whole of
Russia.' As some critics pointed out at the Second Congress, if the
workers were incapable of developing a revolutionary consciousness then nothing was left of the doctrine of Marx that the proletariat was destined as a class by history to bring about the final
socialist revolution. But it was to be many years before the difference was to be fully appreciated between the idea of a revolution
made by the workers themselves and one made by professional
revolutionaries, the party, in their name.

The nature of the forthcoming revolution was much debated
after 1905. Both factions agreed that the constitutional concessions
made by the reluctant Emperor did not amount to a 'bourgeois'
revolution—indeed the fact that the weak Russian middle class
was not prepared to take power in 1905 was only too evident.
Hence, the 'bourgeois' revolution still remained to be completed
—this was generally accepted by all Social Democrats, including
Lenin, and when the autocracy fell in March 1917 this was regarded as the 'bourgeois' revolution. In the course of 1905 Bolsheviks and Mensheviks alike had strained their utmost to increase
revolutionary violence and indeed, through the medium of the
Soviets, appeared to be aiming at power—an insurrection in
Moscow at the end of the year was an attempt to seize power. But
the party lacked both organisation and, in the last resort, popular
support and its failure justified the reproof of some, like
Plekhanov, who argued that the attempt at insurrection had been
premature and mistaken.

After 1906, when the reaction set in, both factions had to re-think their position. The Mensheviks, though far from united, at all events included (as will be seen below) a large wing which followed what looked like an 'orthodox' Marxist line—it advo-cated the need to use all possible opportunities to develop mass worker activity to the maximum, in other words, to develop that conscious and educated working class which would, in the fullness of time, be fit for its historic task. They visualised their own function, in the first place, as supporting the middle-class parties in their assault on the autocracy; and, both before and after this assault, stimulating them to greater revolutionary effort; and in the second place leading the working class to victory when it was ripe to take power—and not before. The Mensheviks were not always consistent and in practice their 'support' of the middle-class parties in the Duma, for example, often differed little from the open hostility of the Bolsheviks.

Lenin's doctrine, especially after 1906, on the coming revolution had the merit of taking into account to a greater extent than the Mensheviks the reality that Russia was still an overwhelmingly peasant country. Lenin envisaged the government which the future revolution would produce as a 'revolutionary democratic dictator-ship of the workers and peasants'. The fact that he included the 'bourgeois' peasants (i.e. bourgeois in Marxist theory) in this coming revolutionary government has often been adduced as evidence that Lenin remained, until 1917, committed to the ortho-dox view of Marx that a bourgeois revolution must precede a socialist revolution. Whatever the truth of this matter there is no doubt that Lenin was visualising a form of government which was very different from the kind of bourgeois democratic regime which Marx had in mind as the training stage for the working class.

What Lenin foresaw was a dictatorship which would break the violent opposition of the bourgeoisie and the landlords to 'the transformations which are immediately and inevitably necessary to the proletariat and the peasantry'; it would radically alter land tenure, introduce complete 'democratisation' and, 'last but not least', spread the flames of revolution to the rest of Europe.

But what Lenin in November 1917 in fact claimed to set up was a 'dictatorship of the proletariat'. The theoretical foundation for the Bolshevik attitude to the state was laid by Lenin in his *State and Revolution*, written in September 1917, but only published some months after the Bolsheviks had seized power. This work analyses the dictatorship of the proletariat—the transition phase from the socialist revolution to the final phase of Communism. For this dictatorship the proletariat requires a proletarian state of its own which it creates after seizing and smashing the existing bourgeois state. Its form of government must be a dictatorship, resting on violence and bound by no law. Since, however, it will be a dictatorship of the enormous majority against a small minority of exploiters, it will have decreasing need to resort to violence. Indeed, as all learn the art of government and acquire the habits of social conformity, the need for a special apparatus of repression disappears and in the fullness of time the state—the proletarian state—will wither away. It was perhaps characteristic that there was only a passing reference in this work to the party—the dictatorship throughout is portrayed as that of a class as a whole. Yet, as Plekhanov had pointed out in one of his earliest pamphlets on Marxism, 'the dictatorship of a class is as far from the dictatorship of a group as heaven is from earth'. It could be argued that the whole conception of the dictatorship of a class is unrealistic and not, in practice, of much meaning. But this is to criticise Marx: it can scarcely serve as an argument for the view that Lenin's dictatorship of the party, which he always identified with the proletariat, is consistent with Marx's interpretation of history.

In March 1917 the Russian monarchy and the old regime collapsed in the largely spontaneous and virtually bloodless February Revolution. The disturbances in the capital began on 23 February (8 March). Both the Bolshevik and the Menshevik underground committees had been thoroughly disorganised by arrests and repressions during the war and played virtually no part in this revolution: for Lenin, in exile in Switzerland, it came as a surprise. But some of the Menshevik 'practicals' played a historic part, for it was due to their efforts that a Soviet came into existence in Petrograd side by side with the Provisional Government set up by the liberal parties in the Duma. It is not possible here to tell the story of events between March 1917 when the monarchy collapsed and 25 October (7 November) 1917 when the Second All-Russian Congress of Soviets voted itself into power and an All-Bolshevik Council of People's Commissars took over the government. But it is necessary to examine three aspects: the policies pursued by the Bolsheviks and the Mensheviks; the reasons for the victory of the Bolsheviks; and the nature of the Bolshevik triumph. For each of these aspects was to exert its influence on the shape of the government which ultimately developed in the country.

The sudden collapse of all authority in March 1917 contained within it the seeds of future developments. For the two institutions which arose side by side—the Provisional Government and the Soviets which soon sprang up all over the country—pursued different aims. To the Provisional Government the revolution seemed an opportunity to prosecute more efficiently a war which the inefficient and decaying monarchy had brought to the verge of disaster. To the Soviets the revolution seemed the immediate promise of better things—peace; and, so far as the peasant soldier in uniform was concerned—land. The Bolsheviks formed a small minority in the Soviets where Mensheviks and Socialist Revolutionaries predominated until August or September. Before long the two organs—the Soviets as spokesman of the masses and the Provisional Government—entered into an uneasy co-operation which always verged on collision. The Provisional Government lacked experience and was reluctant to take stern measures to prevent chaos from overwhelming the country. The Soviets, driven ever further to the left by the pressure from an impatient population little used to the self-discipline that the new democracy required, became more insistent in their demands. The Mensheviks, like the Socialist Revolutionaries, did not demand immediate peace. But their constant demand for 'a just peace without annexations or indemnities' none the less helped to demoralise a weary army. Their policy was to support the Provisional Government to the extent that it favoured a radical policy and a number of Mensheviks eventually entered the Provisional Government.

The policy of the Bolsheviks (at that time led by Stalin and Kamenev) was at first little different from that of the Mensheviks, and indeed there was, right until September or later, among the rank and file a spontaneous movement towards reunification. Lenin's arrival in Petrograd on 16 April caused an immediate change. His declared policy was: fraternisation at the front; no support whatever for the Provisional Government; and all power to the Soviets. The demand that the Soviets should take power was a complete departure from the principle hitherto accepted by Lenin, at any rate in theory, that the proletarian revolution (which is what 'all power to the Soviets' implied) could only take place in

the course of historical development long after the bourgeois
revolution. Lenin's sudden change of tactics disconcerted his
followers at first but not for long. By the summer he had won an
important new ally in the person of Lev Trotsky, a revolutionary
of great fire and brilliance who had for long opposed Lenin and
remained outside the ranks of both Bolsheviks and Mensheviks.
In 1905 Trotsky had advocated 'permanent revolution' which
meant that the socialist and bourgeois revolution should be
telescoped into one—with the socialist revolution beginning as
soon as the bourgeois revolution had taken place. For this un-
orthodox view he had been duly ridiculed by Lenin at the time.
Now their views on the revolution were virtually at one—and
Trotsky's leadership in the decisive months that remained until
seizure of power in November was one of the main factors that
ensured Bolshevik victory.

The reasons for this victory were many and complex and only
some of the main factors can be enumerated. On the Bolshevik
side there was, first, singleness of purpose—the overthrow of the
Provisional Government. The Bolsheviks had the further advantage which no other party possessed: superior organisation,
discipline and armed force—the Red Guard, which the Bolsheviks
had armed and organised, and the Provisional Government was
unwilling, or unable, to suppress. They were reckless in their
promises—bread, peace and land—and had considerable support
among the workers in the capital and in several other cities and in
the sections of the army nearest to the capital. They had ample
funds which they used mainly for disruptive propaganda in the
army. Accusations were levelled by the Provisional Government
that these funds came from German sources. This accusation,
vigorously denied by Lenin at the time, has been substantiated
by the evidence of the archives of the German Foreign Office which
fell into Allied hands during the Second World War.

So far as the Provisional Government was concerned, it failed
in part through lack of support from the socialists to take any
effective measures against the almost open threat of insurrection
by the Bolsheviks until it was too late. It lost the support of those
sections of the army which were anti-Bolshevik and ready to go on
with the war. It delayed the convocation of a Constituent
Assembly and thereby failed to create for itself that legitimacy
which a government requires for survival. It postponed the adoption of any far-reaching measures of land reform and thus failed

to win the confidence of the peasants. Above all, it was handicapped by its determination to fulfil Russia's obligation to its
allies and continue in the war against the Central Powers. By
September, with nowhere to look to for support, the socialist
Prime Minister A. F. Kerensky was forced to choose between sur-
rendering power to a military dictatorship or to the forces of the
left, and chose the latter. From that time on the victory of the
Bolsheviks was only a matter of time.

So far as Lenin was concerned, seizure of power was always
envisaged and described by him as action by his party with the
support of the Red Guard. That his call for 'all power to the
Soviets' was largely a tactical move is evident from the fact alone
that in August when Bolshevik representation was low, the Sixth
Party Congress rejected this slogan and voted instead for seizure
of power by the 'armed people'. Trotsky, with greater vision perhaps, insisted that seizure of power by the Bolsheviks should be
made to coincide with a vote by the forthcoming Congress of
Soviets. In the end, whether by luck or by management, the tactics
of Trotsky prevailed: on 25 October (7 November) the Second
All-Russian Congress of Soviets by its vote set the seal of legality
on a physical seizure of power in the capital which had been
effected hours before by armed force.

After September Bolshevik seats in the Soviets (which were continuously re-elected) had begun to increase and in some they had
majorities. In the Second All-Russian Congress of Soviets of
Workers' and Soldiers' Delegates, the Bolsheviks and their supporters numbered rather more than half of the delegates: the
departure of many of the Mensheviks and Socialist Revolutionaries in protest against what they regarded as a *coup d'état* ensured
Bolshevik predominance. Bolshevik strength in the Congress of
Soviets was rather greater than their support in the country as a
whole because the Congress of Soviets did not represent the
peasants on the land, but only the peasants in soldiers' uniform
and the workers. But the Bolsheviks, as Trotsky had foreseen,
secured the endorsement by the Soviets, which to the radical
masses were the symbol of revolution and of 'democratic' rule;
these early Soviets were amalgams of delegates of various shades
of radicalism and socialism as well as of the more disciplined
Bolsheviks. Lenin and some, but not all, of his followers saw 7
November 1917 as a victory for the vanguard of the proletariat—

the Bolshevik party. But the verdict of the people was delivered on 12/25 November 1917 when the long-delayed elections to the Constituent Assembly were held and the Bolsheviks polled one quarter of the votes recorded.

1. The calendar in use in Russia until February 1918 was thirteen days behind that of western Europe in the twentieth century.

2

FROM THE REVOLUTION TO THE
MODERN SOVIET STATE

The seizure of power by a vote of the Second All-Russian Congress of Soviets on 25 October (7 November) 1917 raised many issues on the nature of that power. By Lenin's theory, since the Bolshevik party alone claimed to represent the victorious class, the proletariat, its right to rule was self-evident and the form in which that rule was to be expressed of secondary importance. To many of his followers the victory had appeared as a victory of the Soviets, and this to them implied a coalition government of all the socialist parties that were represented in the Soviets, since each of them could claim to represent a section of the working class. There was also the further problem that the elections to the Constituent Assembly were due to be held in the last week of November. The Bolsheviks had always been staunch supporters of the Constituent Assembly in words if not in intentions and had repeatedly blamed the Provisional Government for the delay in getting it convened. But the Bolshevik chance of securing a majority in the Constituent Assembly was negligible since the peasants would vote for the party that they were long used to supporting—the Socialist Revolutionaries.

Although desultory discussions on a coalition government began almost immediately after the successful Bolshevik coup they made little progress. In truth, each side in the discussion was divided on the question of a coalition. On the Bolshevik side many of Lenin's followers, especially the rank and file, were genuinely anxious for a coalition with the socialists so as to avoid a civil war. Lenin himself was quite determined that there was to be no coalition, and made it plain to his immediate followers in the Central Committee (on 1/14 November) that the talks on coalition were only intended as a blind in order to gain time while Bolshevik power was consolidating itself in Moscow and in the provinces. In this tactic he had the support of Trotsky, Stalin and a number of other top leaders. The socialist parties in turn were divided on the question. Those more to the left hoped that a coalition would exercise a moderating effect on the Bolsheviks. The majority inclined to the view that by forcibly seizing power the Bolsheviks had forfeited the right to participate in the kind of democratic government which they intended should issue from the revolution. In the event the talks came to nothing. However, Lenin was able to preserve the appearances of moderation without the reality when on 8 December eight Left Socialist Revolutionaries (members of the dissident pro-Bolshevik wing of the Socialist Revolutionary party which had set up as a separate party in November) agreed to join the Council of People's Commissars. It was to prove a short-lived partnership. After an uneasy period of co-existence the Left Socialist Revolutionaries broke with the Bolsheviks in March 1918 as a protest against what they considered the humiliating and, to socialists, dishonourable terms of the Russian peace treaty with Germany and the Central Powers.

In the Bolshevik party there was a short-lived and quite ineffectual revolt during November 1917, in protest both against Lenin's attitude to coalition and against the fact that violent means were used by the Bolsheviks from the start to suppress not only right-wing or even liberal opponents but also critical socialist opponents. A more serious and effective opposition group, headed by Bukharin and known as the Left Communists, grew up in the party originally in protest against the peace terms with the Central Powers. This and the subsequent policy of other socialists will be considered later.

The elections to the Constituent Assembly were held on 12/25 November 1917, less than three weeks after the Bolshevik coup. The Bolsheviks had had no time to interfere with the voting arrangements and did not wish to risk the effect on public opinion of postponing an election which they had themselves so fervently advocated—though the question was mooted. Exhaustive examination of the considerable evidence available leads to the conclusion that the election, though not perfect by the standards of an advanced and experienced democracy, was reasonably free and fairly expressed the opinion of the country. The Bolsheviks polled under one quarter of the forty-one million votes recorded. The remaining votes, apart from some nine and a half million votes cast for the liberals and the national minority factions, went to socialists of all kinds. Of the 707 members elected, 175 were Bolsheviks and 370, an absolute majority, were Socialist Revolutionaries.

The Constituent Assembly opened on 5/18 January 1918. The Bolsheviks had prepared a long declaration endorsing the legislation passed by the Second All-Russian Congress of Soviets on all major issues of power which they demanded that the Constituent Assembly should accept and which in substance left it nothing to do but to approve the organisation of Russian society along lines already determined by the Bolsheviks. When the Assembly rejected this declaration by a large majority the Bolsheviks and Left Socialist Revolutionaries withdrew. Shortly afterwards the Red Guards broke up the meeting and on the following day they forcibly prevented the members from reassembling.

Lenin justified his action at the time and later mainly on two grounds: first, that the elections had taken place too soon after the social transformation effected in November for the voting to reflect it; and secondly, that any election which takes place before the 'workers' (by which he meant the Bolsheviks acting in the name of the workers) are in control of all power in the state is no more than a farce. Whatever one's view of Lenin's theory, there is no doubt his political instinct, that the dispersal of the Assembly would not arouse serious resistance, was right. An attempt by the Socialist Revolutionaries to organise the defence of the Constituent Assembly in Petrograd was half-hearted and ineffectual, in the Bolshevik party there was virtually no protest, while in the country as a whole the incident was treated with indifference. The political immaturity of Russia, as often in her history, favoured the most resolute, if most unscrupulous, political force of the time.

Before many months were over the country was plunged into civil war. For some two and a half years the White armies of the right fought the hastily formed Red Army and were routed. The White side enjoyed the widely publicised but on the whole militarily insignificant support of the British, French and Americans. The Red Army had superior organisation and morale, which were largely due to the ruthless genius of Trotsky, its organiser, and the Bolshevik side also benefited from the political ineptitude of the

White leaders. The Bolsheviks, or Communists as they called themselves after March 1918, came out of the contest more determined
than ever that their cause was right and that their decision to hold
on to power in spite of the fact that they were a minority was
justified. But they discovered by the end of 1920 that the challenge
to the legitimacy of their rule, which remained in abeyance while
the civil war was in progress, now loomed largest on the horizon.

There were a number of reasons for this situation—the most
critical that any government can have to face. The civil war had
brought with it severe hardships for the population—starvation in
many parts of the country, the halving of the population in
Moscow and Petrograd, a doubling of the death rate and a virtual
collapse of industry. While much of this was due to the exigencies
of the war, something was also due to Bolshevik policies. In an
excess of socialist zeal Lenin and the party leaders had introduced
a series of radical measures, known collectively as 'War Communism', which had destroyed both the production of consumer goods
and the existing mechanism of economic exchange. In the villages
the peasants were forcibly deprived of the produce of the land
which, as they were no longer allowed to sell it, they refused to
surrender voluntarily. By the summer of 1920 peasant risings
were beginning to take the form of a guerilla war.

The industrial proletariat was little more satisfied than the
peasants with the results of a revolution made in their name. By
the end of 1920 strikes and demonstrations in Petrograd were
becoming ominous. In March of 1921 the sailors and garrison at
Kronstadt openly rebelled against the Communist regime. The
Kronstadt revolt has often been portrayed by Soviet writers as a
'counter-revolutionary' movement, and condemned accordingly.
But it can only be so described if one identifies—as, of course,
Lenin did—'revolution' and 'Communist Party rule'. The Kronstadt revolutionaries put forward a series of radical demands
which were, perhaps, characteristic of the mood of 1917: what
many at the time had believed to be a victory of the Soviets, critics
of Lenin now said had been traduced into a victory for the
Communist Party. The programme of the Revolutionary Committee of Kronstadt demanded among other things the immediate
re-election of all the Soviets by secret ballot; freedom of speech for
workers, peasants and all left-wing parties; the freeing of all
political prisoners and the abolition of the special Communist
terror detachments in the army and in the villages; freedom for

trade unions; and freedom for the peasants in the use of the land. The reply of the Communist leaders was to send the Red Army to mow down the rebels and to execute the survivors.

Elsewhere political opposition did not reach the same boiling point, though the risk that the Kronstadt mood would spread was certainly real in the spring of 1921. Dissatisfaction with the form which Communist rule had taken was widespread both outside and inside the Communist Party and at least a third of the local Communists supported the rebels in Kronstadt, while many more were 'neutral'. But before examining the mood inside the ruling party it is necessary to look at the political forces outside it.

The White anti-Bolshevik forces, whose aim was the overthrow of the new regime, were by 1921 already scattered and weak. Inside Russia occasional conspiracies were uncovered by the security organs, outside the forces of the anti-Bolshevik emigration were vocal but weak and disorganised. The policy of the Allied Powers was moving towards acceptance of the new Soviet regime as something that had come to stay. On any fair assessment it is impossible to assert that counter-revolution was in 1921 a serious threat.

The two main socialist parties, the Social Democrats (Mensheviks) and the Socialist Revolutionaries, had for long past been leading a *de facto* underground, though officially legal, existence. The Social Democrats had from the first been opposed to any kind of violent as distinct from political opposition to the new regime, though individuals, in defiance of their party, did participate in various violent anti-Communist undertakings. The policy of the party as a whole can in the main be summed up as support of the regime so far as resistance to the White movement was concerned; and free criticism of its policy inside Soviet Russia. The Communists accepted the Social Democrats' not inconsiderable civilian and military aid in the civil war but found their criticism increasingly irksome. As the Communist policy grew more unpopular among the workers, so the Social Democrats, with their dreams of more freedom and their appeals to what they claimed were the orthodox canons of Marxism, grew more popular. The regime retaliated by every kind of administrative repression and discrimination but did not as yet venture to outlaw them. Handfuls of Social Democrats survived in the Soviets and several trade unions were still under their control.

In contrast, the Socialist Revolutionaries, with a long tradition of violent action behind them, took to arms almost from the first. They played an important part on the anti-Bolshevik side in the civil war from the start. But the ill-assorted partnership with the right-wing Whites proved too unpalatable for them. By the end of 1918 they abandoned the partnership and with it their policy of armed resistance. Once again there were individual exceptions, rather more than in the Social Democratic party, and many Socialist Revolutionaries went into exile to try to organise the anti-Soviet front. Inside Russia the party likewise enjoyed a precarious underground existence, reiterating its criticism mainly on its traditional ground, the villages. It would be no more true, on the evidence available, to say that the Socialist Revolutionaries were always responsible for fomenting the risings in the villages than it would be to attribute the Kronstadt rebellion to the activity of the Social Democrats. But it was true that the criticism by these parties of the methods used by the Communists to suppress freedom for all but themselves, and to put into force economic measures which were doctrinaire and ill-advised, contributed to the general growing unrest in the country.

Inside the Communist Party several weak opposition groups were discernible by the end of 1920, which became more insistent in their criticism as the issue of the civil war veered in favour of the regime. The first opposition group, that of the Left Communists led by Bukharin, had long ceased to exist. It had arisen in protest against Lenin's insistence on signing a peace treaty with Germany in March 1918 and demanded what had hitherto been proclaimed as Bolshevik policy—a 'revolutionary war', in other words a guerilla resistance within Russia which was (somewhat romantically) designed to inflame a revolutionary rising of the proletariat in the major industrial countries. The Left Communists subsequently extended their criticism to what they regarded as excessive deviation from the principles of pure Marxist doctrine. This somewhat theoretical and unrealistic movement in the party, which at one time enjoyed considerable support, was routed not by administrative means but by free debate and by the logic of events. By 1920 the two main Communist opposition groupings centred respectively on the trade unions and the Soviet and government machinery. These two groups of Communists—the Workers' Opposition and the Democratic Centralists—while accepting without question the monopoly of power which the party had established against socialist opponents and the means by which it

had been accomplished, resented and criticised the growing centralisation, discipline and stifling of debate inside the party which
had been developing since at least 1919. With little regard for
political logic they desired that freedom for themselves which they
were quite content to deny to others. The Kronstadt rebellion had
a sobering effect on them, implying as it did a threat to the whole
regime which, if it succeeded, would clearly engulf them along with
Lenin and his less critical supporters. This was one of the factors
which enabled Lenin to create a new discipline in his party.

The Tenth Congress of the party met in March 1921, at the time
when the revolt in Kronstadt was in progress. Some two hundred
delegates from the Congress actually took part in the suppression
of the revolt, acting as morale stiffeners to the reluctant troops.
The Tenth Congress was destined to form a watershed in the
history of the Soviet regime. In the economic sphere the time was
ripe for a retreat from doctrinaire policy if ruined industry were to
be restored and if the embattled peasants were to be pacified.
Such a retreat was already under discussion before the events in
Kronstadt and the Congress now adopted the New Economic
Policy. At the outset this was limited to abandoning the system of
forcible requisitioning of the peasants' produce and to allowing
the peasants freedom in the cultivation of the land and in the
marketing of crops. Full state control was retained over foreign
trade, banking and major national industry.

In the political sphere Lenin was faced with two alternatives.
He could either bring about a political reconciliation by sharing
power with the socialists and by permitting freedom of opinion
and discussion inside his own party. Or he could ensure the
monopoly of power for the Communists, but in that case a more
disciplined party had to be created, in order to enable an unpopular
minority to rule in the teeth of national opposition. It was consistent with the whole of his faith and past practice that he should
have chosen the latter course and there is no evidence to support
the view subsequently put about by Stalin's opponents, such as
Trotsky, that the measures he put through at the Congress to this
end were only intended as temporary. The Congress voted by a
large majority to prohibit groups, or factions, within the party, to
restrict criticism in the light of the effect which it was said to have
in helping enemies of the regime, and to tighten and improve the
organisational machinery of the party. The suppression of the
socialists followed soon after but by administrative action, not by

legislation. The main Social Democratic leaders were arrested, but later allowed to emigrate. The Socialist Revolutionary leaders were less fortunate. They were arrested, kept in prison and in the following year, 1922, put on trial in the first of the show trials for which the Soviet regime was later to become famous. It can fairly be said that the Tenth Congress of the party set the pattern of party rule which has in essentials remained in force ever since.

The first few months of the new regime in 1917 was a period of intense legislative activity. Much of the new legislation remained on paper, much of it was not destined to survive the realistic second thoughts dictated more by practical necessity than by revolutionary actions. But out of the spate of this new revolutionary legislation the government took shape and the main stages of its evolution must therefore be looked at.

On 7 November 1917 by their first Declaration, the Second All-Russian Congress of Soviets seized power in the name of the Soviets of Worker, Soldier and Peasant Deputies and proclaimed the Provisional Government overthrown. On the following day a new organ, which was stated to be only provisional until the Constituent Assembly met, was set up—the Council of People's Commissars, invested with 'government power'. This organ, of which Lenin became chairman, was to be responsible to the All-Russian Congress of Soviets and to its Central Executive Committee, which was charged with legislative functions between the meetings of the Congress.

Drastic decrees now poured from the Central Executive Committee, on which the Bolsheviks had an overwhelming majority, and from the Council of People's Commissars. The first decrees, passed on 8 November, were intended respectively as external and internal demonstrations: the decree on Peace offered an immediate armistice to all the belligerents, as a preliminary step to a just peace; the decree on Land nationalised the landlords' estates and granted all agricultural land to the peasants for their use in perpetuity. On 9 November a decree on the press imposed what were stated to be temporary restrictions on the freedom of the newspapers. The eight-hour day was enacted on 11 November, and on the 15th all the non-Russian parts of the country were offered the free choice of their future status including, if they so desired, full autonomy as separate states. On 5 December the entire system of courts of law was swept away and an improvised system devised to replace it. Widespread nationalisation and centralised economic management were adopted early in 1918. The chaos which war and revolution had generated, the imminent civil war and the increasing resistance of the population to Bolshevik rule would alone have prevented the implementation in practice of this far-reaching programme. In effect government took the form of administrative action by the Bolshevik leaders at the centre and by the Bolsheviks on the spot, without much regard for legal forms. The setting up of the Extraordinary Commission for Combating Counter-Revolution and Sabotage, the *Cheka*, with its numerous local sub-commissions, on 19 December 1917 (the precursor of the powerful organisation for internal security which under different names has survived in the Soviet Union ever since) provided the party with strong centralised machinery for applying its arbitrary powers and preserving its rule by terror.

For general administration the party leaders had to rely on the network of Soviets in which all power had been vested by decrees of 7 and 8 November. It was true that the Bolsheviks very soon secured complete predominance in all Soviets within the area of Russia to which the new regime extended—correcting, where necessary, the results of the ballot box by force. But the party was ill-equipped with central machinery to enforce discipline and obedience on its growing membership and by 1919 signs of anarchy and individualism were apparent. In order to correct this trend the party machinery was considerably strengthened in 1919. A smaller Political Bureau was set up to enable the party leaders to meet more frequently for policy decisions than had been possible so long as the sole governing organ of the party was the larger Central Committee. More important still, the party's still rudimentary Secretariat was considerably strengthened and reorganised. Details about these organs of the party will be found in the next chapter. The stricter discipline of the party, which many members were beginning so strongly to resent by 1921, dates from these reforms.

The first Constitution was adopted by the Fifth All-Russian Congress of Soviets on 10 July 1918. The Third Congress, on 28 January 1918, with the Constituent Assembly out of the way, had laid down some of the principles of the new Constitution—in particular the federal nature of what was now to be called the Russian Soviet Federal Socialist Republic (RSFSR); and the vesting of all local, as distinct from federal, powers in the Soviets of those areas

which were inhabited by non-Russian nationals. The Constitution
finalised this by defining the respective powers of the federal and
local Soviets. But this question as yet remained an academic one.
At this date the parts of the former Russian Empire in which
nationalist feelings were strongest were not under the sway of the
new regime. Some had achieved complete independence (such as
the Baltic provinces and Finland); others formed part of the
theatre of the civil war outside Bolshevik control.

The Constitution of the RSFSR recited at length the faith and
political aims of the new regime. It also enacted what is described
as 'real' freedom of press, meeting and association for the workers
and poor peasants which it stated was ensured by providing these
classes with the facilities for publishing newspapers and for
assembly and association. The supreme legislature was to be the
All-Russian Congress of Soviets elected indirectly by the town and
rural Soviets on a franchise which was weighted in favour of the
urban population. Certain classes considered hostile to the revolution were completely disenfranchised. The provisions were similar
for the election of the local Soviets where the voting was, however, to be direct. At the centre the All-Russian Central Executive
Committee of the Soviets was charged with supreme power
between sessions of the All-Russian Congress and the Council of
People's Commissars was entrusted with the 'general direction' of
public affairs. The local Soviets were also provided with an
executive committee. There is no mention, in this Constitution, of
the Communist Party, or of the *Vecheka*.

In spite of the formal declaration of the right of the national
minorities to determine their own future, even if this involved
secession from the new Russia, such in fact was never the policy of
the party. There was a long tradition of centralisation in the
Bolshevik party, and no autonomy had ever been conceded to the
Bolshevik movements which had sprung up among the various
national minorities of the Russian Empire. After the revolution,
in the Programme adopted by the party in March 1919, the party
reaffirmed the principle of national self-determination, including
the right of secession, but made it clear that it was the hope if not
the intention of the party that the influence of the Communists in
all the areas inhabited by non-Russians, at that date outside the
control of the new regime, would prove strong enough to induce
a movement for reunification. The Programme proposed for the
future a federal union of states organised on the Soviet pattern

'as one of the transitional forms on the path to complete unity'; and declared that the question of who, in any particular case, must be regarded as the bearer of the will of any nation on the issue of separatism, must be decided 'according to the historic stage of development of that nation'—in practice, by the party in Moscow.

In the event, as Soviet rule was consolidated in the course of the civil war, the party succeeded by a combination of persuasion and force in reintegrating many portions of the former Russian Empire. In the case of social-democratic Georgia, for example, a rising was fomented by the Communists in 1921 in order to justify a military invasion—both acts in open violation of express provisions of a treaty of 7 May 1920. The RSFSR failed in its efforts in the less vulnerable Baltic states and in Poland. In the course of extending Communist control, by one means or another, to the reintegrated territories, the party pursued a policy of centralisation and indeed in some measure of Russification, putting down in the process manifestations of nationalism, which also appeared among the Communist Party members of the national minorities.

By the end of 1922 the time was considered ripe to give final recognition to a reintegration which was already a fact. The plan for union was completed by December 1922, and approved by the Tenth Congress of Soviets on 26 December. Three days later articles of Union were signed by Communist representatives of the only republics concerned at the time—the RSFSR, the Ukraine, Belorussia and Transcaucasia (the latter was a union consisting of Georgia, Armenia and Azerbaijan). A draft of a new Constitution was worked out after a good deal of discussion, approved by the Central Executive Committee on 6 July 1923 and ratified by the Second All-Union Congress of Soviets on 31 January 1924.

The Constitution of the new Union of Soviet Socialist Republics (USSR) recited the articles of Union entered into by the Soviet republics, and looked forward to the day when the workers of all countries in the world would be united in one World Socialist Soviet republic. It also recited the powers of the Union, which were fairly extensive, and laid down that each Union republic retained its full autonomy in all fields not expressly assigned to the Union and above all its right freely to secede. The new supreme legislature, the Congress of Soviets of the Union of Soviet Socialist Republics, and the Central Executive Committee of the Congress of Soviets which was to exercise legislative powers between sessions of the Congress, were both as before to be elected.

The Constitution of 1924 also set up a new system of law courts and a revised system of state security under central control—the United State Political Directorate, usually known by its initials in Russian—OGPU.

Once again, the Constitution made no mention of the party. Yet, with the centralised party increasing its hold over the state machinery throughout the country, even the limited autonomy allowed to the republics in the constitution could easily be over-ridden. In particular, it was already inconceivable by 1924 that any attempt at secession on the part of a Union republic could be treated as anything other than counter-revolution—a show trial of a nationalist Tartar Communist in 1923 had already established this. This second Constitution remained in force until 1936.

The New Economic Policy (NEP) of concession to the peasants' traditional property instincts seems to have been intended by Lenin in 1921 as a long-term measure—as he put it, one of generations but not of centuries. He seems from his last writings (in 1922 and 1923) to have been anxious to undo the harm that had been done by the ill-considered and over-zealous measures of doctrinaire 'War Communism'; to reconcile the peasants whose resentment had been aroused by the fact that while some land had been given to them with one hand its produce had been forcibly confiscated with the other; and to make possible in the course of a long period of social peace between peasants and proletariat the adoption of socialist measures by voluntary acceptance which compulsion had so far signally failed to achieve. Lenin did not live to guide his new economic policy himself. By 1923 he was already too ill to work and he died on 21 January 1924.

The consequences of NEP were both economic and political and events in both fields must be followed in order to understand subsequent developments. On the economic side, the relaxation of NEP certainly brought about a revival both of agriculture and of industry and of the general standard of living, which reached something like the 1913 level by around 1927. However, this comparative prosperity, although it redounded to the benefit especially of the peasants, failed to produce a sufficient accumulation of capital for the development of heavy industry, which had made a rapid start in Russia in the decade before the First World War. While all the Communist leaders were agreed on the need to develop heavy industry there was considerable disagreement on the methods by which this could be achieved. Those who had some claim to consider themselves the closest followers of the dead Lenin's views, such as Bukharin, regarded the duty to preserve peace and harmony between social classes, on which Lenin had laid so much stress, as paramount. They were prepared to sanction some fiscal means for restricting the growth of the peasants' income but they considered the main means of accumulating capital for the development of heavy industry to be the extensive development of consumer industry which would induce the peasant to part with his profits in return for consumer goods. It was probably also the case that Bukharin still hoped to attract foreign loans: hitherto the intransigent attitude of the Communist government to the debts of the imperial government and its refusal to honour legal obligations had frightened off potential foreign investors.

The left-wing leaders of the party had never been reconciled to NEP which they regarded as a retreat from socialism. They believed in the need for a more radical, planned attempt to force capital out of the peasants in order to develop heavy industry, even if this involved a departure from the central idea of NEP—the social harmony insisted on by Lenin. At this point the political element enters into the question. Since Lenin's death Stalin had rapidly been building up, through his control of the party's central Secretariat, a position of enormous power in the party, and therefore in the country. His most serious rival from the start of his rise to power, during Lenin's lifetime in 1922, was Trotsky. Trotsky was not only a more colourful and talented personality, but had the advantage of having played an outstanding part in 1917 and in the civil war and of having been generally considered Lenin's choice as successor. It was against Trotsky, therefore (who proved himself very unskilful in the arts of political intrigue), that Stalin directed his blows in the first instance. Since the 'left' advocates of more rapid industrialisation and of the use of sterner methods against the peasants were for the most part followers of Trotsky, it was necessary for Stalin to seek support from the right-wing leaders until such time as he could settle his scores with the left. He therefore supported their policies in turn.

By the end of 1927 Trotsky and his followers had been completely outplayed and outwitted, and were sent off into remote banishment early in 1928. For Trotsky this was to form the first stage towards years of exile, and murder by Stalin's agents in 1940

Stalin now inaugurated the rapid industrialisation of the country, which involved enforced extraction of the capital and labour required from the peasant. This was, of course, a complete reversal of what Stalin had been advocating, in opposition to the 'left' leaders, since 1921. Now that the 'left' leaders were out of the way, if was safe for him to adopt a policy which, while closer to Trotsky's views than to those of the 'right', went a good deal further in its free use of force and in its pace than anyone on the left had ever contemplated. As the new policy evolved it became apparent that it entailed, first the driving of the peasants into collective farms in the teeth of desperate resistance and a loss of life estimated in millions; and secondly, an attempt to achieve a rate of industrial growth which exceeded any planning figures which had ever been put forward by any responsible economist.

This is not the place to discuss either the 'necessity' or the 'justification' of Stalin's policy, in so far as such questions have any real meaning. Serious arguments can be brought forward to show that alternative methods involving less human cost might have achieved the same or even better industrial results. It is certainly true that Soviet agriculture had not recovered thirty years later from the damage inflicted on it by Stalin's 'third revolution', as it came to be called. On the other hand, the system of rule inherited by Stalin was certainly better adapted to methods of command and intrigue than to methods of responsible co-operation. If it was true that Stalin's policy, in addition to its economic effects, had the, for him, convenient result of eliminating all his political opponents and his potential rivals for power, it was also true that the system devised by Lenin could really only work effectively where one man was in undisputed command.

Whatever the verdict of history on Stalin may ultimately be it can be safely asserted that to attempt to assess his stature solely in economic or solely in political terms, when his policy was so completely unified as a whole, is to do violence to all the known facts. His sudden desertion of the 'right', the champions of Lenin's policy of social peace, involved logically the political destruction of Bukharin and those who thought like him. (Physical destruction of the leaders of both right and left had to be delayed for some years until Stalin felt strong enough to carry it out.) The violence of the economic and agricultural policy, the filling up of the concentration camps, the transformation of economic critics into counter-revolutionaries, the branding of those who failed to achieve the physically impossible as saboteurs, the swelling of the powers and numbers of the security forces—all these drove the political development of the USSR along logically predictable lines, or at any rate into a logically explicable pattern. Thus the main features of the whole period of 1929 to 1939 in Soviet history are closely linked: collectivisation of the peasants, industrialisation and the great purges of 1936–8. The violence of the economic policy and its defiance of all genuine political opinion in the party logically demanded the elimination of those who held genuine political opinion—those described as the left and the right. Those who formed Stalin's main support in the execution of his policy were for the most part men who followed him out of fear rather than respect, or out of personal ambition rather than political conviction, perhaps most frequently because they were too deeply involved to turn back. Many of them were newcomers to the party for whom the purges made room.

But it was not enough for Stalin to find loyal executors of his policy. The early years of the reversal of NEP—the years of the collectivisation of the farms and of the first Five Year Plan—were years of terror and suffering for most of the population of the country. By 1934, with the worst over—or so it seemed—a mood of reconciliation seems to have swept the country and the party. The old oppositionists of left and right were still alive—a symbolic reconciliation with them now took place at the Seventeenth Congress of the party. Rumour has it that changes were contemplated at the top which were designed to diminish Stalin's great authority—it was certainly true that in 1934 Stalin was officially described as 'Secretary' of the party, but no longer as 'General Secretary'. His rumoured successor, Kirov, the First Secretary of the Leningrad Party Organisation, was murdered at the end of 1934 in circumstances which certainly suggested Stalin's complicity. Years later, in 1956, Stalin's complicity was virtually admitted by his successor in office.

Yet the national blood-bath into which Russia was to be plunged in the middle of 1936 still held off, in spite of the limited wave of terror which followed upon the murder of Kirov. Evidently the forces in the party which were working for reconciliation were still strong enough to hold off the assault which some of the evidence suggests Stalin would have liked to unleash in 1934. It was perhaps primarily with the intention of playing for time that Stalin agreed in 1935 to the setting up of a commission for drafting a new Constitution. Leading oppositionists (later to be shot as traitors) were members of the drafting commission, and the new Constitution certainly contained provisions for safeguarding the rights of the individual which had not in practice been protected for many years. Yet by the time the new Constitution (discussed in chapter 4) was adopted, on 5 December 1936, the terrifying great purge was in full swing. It reigned unrestrained until 1938, claiming as victims millions of people in every walk of life and in every part of the country.

No one in his senses could believe the allegations of sabotage, treason, espionage, counter-revolutionary conspiracy and the like which were used by Stalin and his henchmen in the legal and security apparatus in order to carry out this systematic massacre. A few years after Stalin's death his successors were openly admitting that all these charges were trumped up, that confessions were extracted by torture, and that even the rudiments of legality were ignored. However, it would be a mistake to dismiss the events of these years as symptoms of insanity. Stalin derived certain solid gains from his cruel policy so far as his own position was concerned. By thus enhancing the 'class war'—as it was officially called—he did at any rate put an end to the trend towards reconciliation in the ranks of the party, which could have proved, probably would have proved, disastrous to him, the prime author of the period of strife. By executing or sending to the forced labour camps some three-quarters of his colleagues on the Central Committee and an even larger proportion of the military high command, he did at all events ensure the unswerving loyalty and support of the few who were not executed—loyalty and support, that is, so long as he was alive. They were not slow to blacken his reputation after his death. By virtually wiping out the old generation of Communists (including every one of Lenin's closest collaborators before and after the revolution), and filling the party and state administration with newcomers who stepped into dead men's shoes and owed everything to Stalin, he created a loyal support for himself for his own lifetime. His work even stood the test of war—though only just and in large measure as the result of the brutal policy of Hitler, who, so far as the population of Russia was concerned, seemed to surpass even Stalin in his inhumanity.

The achievement of the Soviet people in recovering from the initial attack by Germany and in defeating the forces of Hitler was outstanding. If it was true that Stalin and the party were to blame for a policy which resulted in a failure to prepare for war, it was also true that both Stalin and the party provided necessary leadership in the conduct of the war. Yet the motive force during those years of suffering and heroism was patriotism. The rigours of the regime were relaxed during the war and doctrine laid aside in favour of nationalist and even religious appeals. When the war was over the old regime returned in all its pristine severity.

A vital feature of Stalin's rule was the extension of control to all aspects of economic, social, intellectual and cultural life. It was, of course, an inherent part of Lenin's conception that the party, the vanguard, should exercise control—if only to prevent the predominance of that 'spontaneity' in which Lenin saw so great a danger. But Stalin was waging war on the party as much as on any other part of the nation. Thus it came about that his system of total control tended to transcend the lines of party control—he worked through his personal control of the security forces and through henchmen of one sort and another, who in time created the largest internal system of espionage which had hitherto been known in any society. The efficacy of such an overall system of terror of this kind is high, but of limited duration. It probably has to be repeated once in a generation. Thus it appears that on the eve of his death on 5 March 1953 Stalin was contemplating a repeat performance, another mammoth purge. Whether his death was natural or not is impossible to say on the evidence: what is quite certain is that for very many people it came only just in time.

Since Stalin's death the Soviet Union has undergone considerable change. Opinion of qualified observers is divided on the question whether the country still remains in essentials the totalitarian police state which Stalin built on Lenin's foundations. The fifteen years which have elapsed since March 1953 can be divided into three periods. Until 1955 there was a short period of 'collective leadership': the offices of First Secretary of the CPSU Central Committee and Chairman of the Council of Ministers of the USSR were held respectively by N. S. Khrushchev and G. M. Malenkov. But even during this period the growing ascendancy of the party machine was evident. The second period (which lasted until October 1964), that of party ascendancy over all aspects of national life, may probably be dated from the fall of Malenkov in February 1955, even though the two key offices still remained separated, and Khrushchev did not take over the office of Chairman of the Council of Ministers of the USSR until March 1958.

During these intervening three years Khrushchev successfully pursued a struggle against the so-called 'anti-party group'. This description, applied mainly to Malenkov, Kaganovich and Molotov, and those who became identified with them, was true to the extent that they appear to have resisted the growing encroachment of the party apparatus in the sphere of government and administration. Their main offence was, no doubt, their resistance to Khrushchev's policies and ambitions. Be that as it may, by the middle of 1957 these surviving leaders of the Stalin era (of whom Khrushchev himself was, of course, also one) were driven from the Praesidium of the Central Committee into oblivion, with various degrees of opprobrium, and with no opportunity of publicly stating their own case. Marshal Zhukov, who had supported Khrushchev at the crucial moment in his conflict with the anti-party group, was driven from office and all positions of honour a few months later—a salutary warning to any other leading soldier who might be tempted in future to adopt the role of kingmaker: and a striking illustration of the truism that there is no room for gratitude in politics.

Yet it would be quite erroneous to regard the era of Khrushchev's real predominance (June 1957–October 1964) solely in terms of personal ambition. He was a great innovator in two respects (three, if his short-lived reform of industry, which will be discussed in a later chapter, is included): in advancing the power and influence of the party and its apparatus, which had stagnated during the period of Stalin's personal despotism, and in facing with a degree of determination, for which he deserves (but is unlikely to receive) the gratitude of millions of his countrymen, the need to disavow Stalin's reign of terror, inhumanity, injustice, violence and deceit.

Khrushchev's reforms of the organisation of the party, and indeed his reform of industry, which were primarily designed to make control by the party apparatus more effective at all points in the national life, proved short-lived. As will be seen in later chapters, they did not long outlast his own downfall on 15 October 1964. Indeed the primary desire of his successors seemed to be to keep party intervention in all economic matters down to a minimum, and to delimit more carefully the respective spheres of the party and the government apparatus. It was for this reason that the offices of First (since April 1966, General) Secretary of the Party and Chairman of the Council of Ministers were once again divided, after Khrushchev's resignation, between two men of ostensibly equal standing—L. I. Brezhnev and A. I. Kosygin. Yet not all of Khrushchev's reform of the party has vanished without trace. Perhaps his most important service to it was to restore its position in the life of the country as something more than the dictator's personal cohort of myrmidons—which is what the party apparatus often appeared to be under Stalin. Regularity and order were restored in the functioning of party organs. It would be an exaggeration to say that full and free discussion became possible in the party: caution, formalism and careful direction of debate from above still remained the rule. Party elections under Khrushchev were as rigidly controlled from the centre as before (and since). Nevertheless, it is true to say that under Khrushchev the party began to approximate more to an organ for the formation of élite opinion than at any time since the early twenties. This part of Khrushchev's reforms has at all event survived his personal eclipse.

The most momentous change effected by Khrushchev was his repudiation of Stalin. The first move was against the security service (see chapter 8): a series of arrests and executions (with scant regard for legal niceties) of high security officials in the course of 1953 and 1954 had the effect of reducing this service to the role of the executive arm of the central party organs. This development must have pleased Khrushchev's colleagues since henceforward it would be difficult for any one man to do what Stalin had done, to use the police organs as his personal instrument. (However, as First Secretary of the party Khrushchev still retained the dominant influence over the KGB until such time as it transferred its allegiance overnight to the next Secretary in line, Brezhnev.) The arbitrary powers of the security organs were considerably curtailed: the millions of their victims in the concentration camps were gradually released, and some rehabilitated, if necessary posthumously.

At the Twentieth Congress of the CPSU, in February 1956, Khrushchev delivered his famous attack, in secret session, on the period of the 'cult of personality'. It was true that the attack was carefully circumscribed so as to limit it to the period after 1934 when Stalin's main attack was being directed against party members, and to leave intact Stalin's reputation for the previous period of forced collectivisation, when his attack was being delivered against the peasants. It was also true that

Khrushchev's exposure of Stalin fell far short of a true or complete statement of all the facts which have long been known to informed students outside the Soviet Union, indeed to all who were not too blinded by bias to see. Nevertheless, the impact of Khrushchev's 'secret speech' (which was widely circulated inside the Soviet Union and was soon published abroad) was devastating: the ferment which it started is far from exhausted today, fourteen years later. In spite of attempts to keep 'liberalisation' within strict limits, the degree of intellectual freedom which 'destalinisation' has brought in its train cannot be compared with anything that has happened in the Soviet Union since the period of NEP in the twenties.

In a certain sense Khrushchev fell a victim to his own policies. His resignation on 15 October 1964, whatever the many reasons which may have induced his successors to force it, was certainly only made possible through the support of the party apparatus, and through the readiness of the KGB to abandon him. In spite of his genuine efforts to increase the influence of the party, Khrushchev's policies had been far from popular either in the KGB or in many sections of the party apparatus. As often as not the authority of the officials of these organisations depended solely on their ability to behave like 'little Stalins', and this authority Khrushchev had undermined.

The dual role by Brezhnev and Kosygin inaugurated the third period since Stalin's death: the period of real collective leadership (as distinct from the fake collective leadership between 1953 and 1955) by the party and government leaders in joint harness, and in apparent harmony. For the first few years after Khrushchev's fall the indications were that the two halves of the collective leadership were endeavouring to respect each other's preserve, and to avoid a repetition of the traditional Soviet form of power struggle. By 1973 it was evident that the CPSU was becoming the dominant partner. For example, foreign policy, which for some years after 1964 was under the control of the Chairman of the Council of Ministers, was now clearly dominated by the General Secretary of the CPSU. By 1977 this domination had, if anything, increased. The offices of General Secretary of the Council of Ministers still remained divided. But the election of the General Secretary to the additional post of State President suggested that his political supremacy had been recognised. In the sphere of planning and the management of industry fundamental changes were made which will be described in a later chapter. Though there has been considerable change of emphasis designed to keep 'liberalisation' under stricter control, there has been no return to 'Stalinism' in the sense of unbridled terror.

Is the Soviet Union in 1977 still a totalitarian state? Certainly, a great deal of arbitrary power is still wielded both by the state and by the party with impunity: there is no independent judiciary, the spoken and printed word are strictly controlled, and every man's livelihood, if not his life and liberty, is at the mercy of the state. The opportunity for the ordinary citizen to influence policy is negligible. This said, so much has happened since Stalin died that it may prove very difficult to reverse the process to which Khrushchev gave such a powerful initial impetus. The open dispute with China has driven a coach and four through the doctrine of the infallibility and unity of Marxism-Leninism. The empire of satellites built up by Stalin with the aid of force and fraud has twice been forcibly reminded that the Soviet Union intends to be master—in Hungary in 1956 and in Czechoslovakia in 1968. Even so, Stalin's stranglehold may prove as difficult to restore abroad as at home. Talk of legality, of the evils of the period of the 'personality cult', the successful assertion of their intellectual independence by the scientists and with much more limited success by the writers, the widening breach in the 'iron curtain'—all this, and much more, may have started the Soviet Union along a path of evolution of which the end cannot yet be foreseen.

3

THE COMMUNIST PARTY

The party which now exercises leadership in the USSR is known as the Communist Party of the Soviet Union (CPSU). Until 1952 the party retained in its title a reference to the traditional name 'Bolshevik', dating from the split between the two sections of Russian social democracy which took place in 1903—All-Russian Communist Party (Bolsheviks) from 1918 until 1925, and All-Union Communist Party (Bolsheviks) until 1952.

The total strength of the party in February 1976 was 15,694,187, including candidate or probationer members. Since the party has always claimed to be an élite of the best citizens its aim has never been maximum expansion but nearly always selective recruitment. Its growth has been far from uniform since it came to power in 1917. Numbering less than a quarter of a million at the time when it seized power in November 1917, it included less than half a million on 1 January 1923, having undergone both purging and intensive recruitment. Five years later, on 1 January 1928, the total strength had reached 1,304,471.

Membership now rose steadily to over three and a half million by 1933. But in the following years the drastic upheavals to which the party was subjected during the purges were reflected in the membership figures. By 1 January 1937 total membership stood at just under two million, and its total strength was much the same two years later, although recruitment, suspended at the beginning of 1933, had been resumed at the end of 1936. All in all, the number of those affected by the purges of the party which took place between 1933 and 1938 can be estimated at somewhere between one and a half and two million. Membership rose again after 1939. In February 1941, on the eve of the outbreak of war between Germany and Russia, total strength was 3,876,885. Recruitment was encouraged during the war, and by 1 January 1945 membership totalled 5,760,369. Expansion was now slowed down, and the total increase by 1 October 1952 was just over a million and in the following four years less than half a million. Since 1965 the party has been growing at the average rate of 450,000 a year. This annual increase is, in proportion, much greater than the natural annual increase of population. It can therefore be assumed that the party leaders are not yet satisfied that an optimum size of the party has been reached.

The social composition of the party over the years is not easy to determine with certainty. For many years no official data are available. Besides, even where official data are available, the political controversy which has often been associated with the social composition of what was supposed to be the vanguard of the ruling class, the proletariat, renders much of the data unreliable. Until 1933, when recruitment was suspended, the official policy of the party in admitting new members was to give preference to workers and working peasants in order to create a party which corresponded to the theory which it claimed to embody. But even during this early period the policy did not work out in practice. According to official data two-thirds of the party in 1923 was made up of 'proletarian elements'. However, a closer examination of all available data on the actual occupation of party members suggests that even at that date at least two-thirds of all party members were in fact employed in positions of authority. In 1928 nearly half of all party members were engaged in non-manual occupations.

Since 1936 the policy of the party has been to recruit those who are considered most suitable in all walks of life and, with the removal of even the theoretical preference for workers, the white collar element in the party has tended to increase. In 1957 this element could be reliably estimated at around 70% of the total membership. Since then there has been a renewed attempt to broaden the base of the party, possibly in an effort to carry into practice a change which was taking place in theory. For by 1961 the party was no longer being described as the 'vanguard of the proletariat' but as the 'vanguard of the Soviet people'. According to official data published in 1976 the social composition of the party was as follows: workers 41·6%, collective farmers 13·9%, 'employees and all others' 44·5%. It was claimed in official data published in July 1961 that only forty-six per thousand of all Communists engaged in production were in managerial posts. Nearly two-thirds of the third category consisted of managers of economic enterprises and specialists in various branches of science and culture. How reliable these figures are is another matter— official statistics of this kind have, in fact, repeatedly proved to be worth but little. Nor is there any lack of evidence at lower levels which is quite inconsistent with the official classification. For example, in May 1963 a party committee, said to be 'typical', in a Kazakhstan state farm, 107 strong in all, was said to consist of 45 administrators; 41 working in crop production as foremen, tractor driver or accountants; and 21 working in the livestock section. Of the last category only two are real manual workers—a milkmaid and a swineherd. No reliable information is available on the social origins, as distinct from occupations, of party members. At present (1977), as the result of the social upheavals which have taken place, it is safe to assume that the overwhelming majority of party members, including those in positions of authority, are of peasant or worker origin. But until inroads were made on the older Bolsheviks as the result of the purges of the thirties, at any rate, the leading stratum of party officials was to a large extent of middle-class origin.

The ethnic composition of the party is not yet strictly proportional to the numbers of every particular national group, though efforts have been made in past years to step up recruitment of some of the nationals such as Ukrainians whose representation remained under strength. Figures for Jews, published in 1976, gave the percentage of Jewish party members as 1·9%, which is quite high in relation to the proportion of Jews in the total population – probably 1%. Until the purges of the thirties the number of Jews in the party was well in excess proportionately to the total Jewish population and many Jews were in positions of authority in the party hierarchy. Whatever the position today as regards the rank and file of the party, a Jew in a position of authority in the party is a rare exception. There is still a heavy concentration of party membership in the large cities. Thus, on the basis of information provided by the republican party congresses of 1961, it was evident that more than a fifth of all party members (some 2,118,000) reside in the seven largest cities in the country. The population of these cities, however, is only about 7% of the total population of the country.

The party is predominantly—nearly four-fifths—male, and young. By January 1965 three-quarters of all party members had been born and bred under Soviet power, in other words they were men and women for whom the revolution and the civil war were legends. By 1 January 1966, 53 % of all party members were under forty, and a further 24·9 % were between forty-one and fifty. At the upper levels of the party hierarchy of officials men over fifty still predominate. But the younger generation predominates among secretaries of urban and rural district party organisations, and to a lesser extent among secretaries of republican and regional organisations. It was, perhaps, symptomatic of the trend to encourage the new men knocking at the door that among the delegates to the All-Union Party Congress held in 1961 the proportion of delegates under forty as well as the proportion of members who had joined the party after 1946 had doubled when compared with the Congress held in 1959. The same trend was observable at the republican party congresses held in 1961 when compared with those held in 1959.

The party is governed by its Statute or Rules. These must be adopted by the party Congress, and have been frequently revised since the first Rules were adopted in 1898. The Rules at present in force were adopted by the Twenty-Second Congress in October 1961, and revised by the Twenty-Third Congress in March–April 1966 and again by the Twenty-Fourth Congress in March–April 1971.

The 'guiding principle' of the party, according to its Rules, is 'democratic centralism'. This is stated to comprise: the election of all leading party organs from top to bottom; periodic accounting by party organs to their own party organisations and to higher party organs;[1] strict party discipline and the subordination of the minority to the majority; and the unconditionally binding force on lower organs of the decisions of higher organs (article 19). In order to ascertain the extent of democracy in the party (which can be described in any political party as the right freely to debate and freely to elect), certain other provisions in the Rules must be noted, which are not always consistent one with another.

The preamble recites the fundamental law of the party: 'monolithic' unity in ideas and in organisation, and the prohibition of all 'factions' and groups; and among the duties of a party member is

listed the duty to use all his endeavours 'to strengthen the ideological and organisational unity of the party' (article 2).

As against this, the party member has under the Rules certain
important rights of debate at party meetings and in the party
press: he has the right fully to discuss and to make proposals
about 'questions of policy and the practical activity' of the party
until such time as a decision has been reached; the unrestricted
right fully to criticise any Communist, irrespective of the post
which he occupies; and the right to make representations, if need
be up to the level of the Central Committee, and to demand an
answer (article 3). It is also stated to be the 'inalienable' right of the
party member to engage in 'free and business-like' discussion of
the policy of individual party organisations and of the party as a
whole, and there are provisions for discussion on a nationwide
scale in certain instances, with safeguards against the formation
of groups (article 27).

As regards elections, the Rules nowhere proclaim that elections
should be free, though the right to elect and to be elected to party
organs is allowed to every party member (article 3). As against
this, it is the duty of every party member 'steadfastly to carry into
effect the party line on the selection of cadres for their political
and practical qualifications', and to show 'irreconcilable' resistance to any attempt to violate 'Leninist principles' in the selection
of cadres (article 2). Elections (except of party officials) are by
secret vote, and voting is for one candidate at a time. All members
of the party organisation have the 'unlimited' right to criticise any
candidate for office. A candidate who has received more than half
of the votes of those present at the meeting is deemed elected
(article 24). These principles apply to all party elections—that is
to say, of committees, of delegates to conferences and congresses,
and of secretaries. At the same time the Central Committee is
charged with the general duty of 'ensuring the selection and distribution of leading cadres' (article 35) which it exercises through
the Secretariat (article 39); and secretaries of rural and urban
district committees must be confirmed in their office by the next
highest party organisation (article 49).

The Rules are thus an amalgam of democratic and centralistic
principles but there is little doubt about which of the two principles has generally prevailed throughout the history of the party.
There have been few occasions, since 1921 at any rate, when the
party leaders have been unable both to keep discussion of policy

within the limits which they considered desirable, and to ensure the election only of those members of committees, officials and delegates of whom they approve; as well as to secure the dismissal of those of whom they disapprove. Official policy of the party is in practice seldom, if ever, criticised until the leaders responsible for that policy have fallen from power, unless the leadership is temporarily divided and one faction successfully instigates public criticism of the other. Except at the lowest levels of the party hierarchy, where genuine criticism of a local official or committee occasionally takes place, criticism of party leaders does not take place unless inspired from the top. As for elections, the central Secretariat, as will be seen, maintains a special department for personal records and for the selection of leading 'cadres' throughout the party. At every election a representative of the party authority next in the hierarchy is present and, with some exceptions, and then only at the lowest levels, is successful in putting through the election of the candidates of whom he approves, and of whom he knows his superiors in the hierarchy to approve. Such is the picture that appears from the extensive information available in the party press on life in the party.

Why does the party member not prove more assertive of the rights which he enjoys under the Rules? Much of the answer lies in the tradition of the party—the man who gets on is the man who takes no risks and keeps a weather eye on authority. Penalties for insubordination have often been savage in the past and can still be pretty severe. Expulsion from the party, or even a reprimand, can have immediate disastrous consequences for an individual where all employment is controlled by the state, and the state in turn is controlled by the party. Above all, the absence of any kind of independent or semi-judicial organ for adjudicating between the rank and file member and the central authorities of the party means that the dice are loaded against the party member who has once fallen foul of authority.

The organisation of the party is both territorial and functional. The territorial organisation is roughly parallel to the administrative sub-division of the country (for which see chapter 5). At the All-Union level the organisation comprises the All-Union Congress and the permanent organs of party administration, which are described below. The next tier is formed by the party organisations of the fourteen Union republics (all the Union republics with the exception of the RSFSR), of the six areas and of the regions—in which for party purposes are included the autonomous republics and the autonomous regions (see chapter 4). These totalled 148 in January 1976. The last tier is composed of ten circuit organisations, 813 city organisations, 571 urban and 2,857 rural district organisations. The functional organisation of the party is composed of 390,387 primary party organisations formed at industrial enterprises, state and collective farms and government, educational, cultural, scientific and trading institutions.

Two points should be noted. First, that the largest and most important Union republic, the RSFSR, has no party organisation separate from the All-Union organisation. Secondly, that the party organisations of the Union republics are in no sense national parties, but branches of the All-Union party, subject to central discipline and direction like any other subordinate party organisation. This principle of centralisation, cutting across the national divisions of the country, has always been cardinal in party policy. It follows from this that such administrative or national autonomy as exists within each of the Union republics (see chapters 4 and 7) can only exist within the framework of the control exercised by a highly centralised All-Union party.

According to the party Rules, the supreme organ of the party is the All-Union Congress. The Congress elects a Central Committee and a Central Revision Commission. The Central Committee elects a Political Bureau (Politburo) and a Secretariat. The Central Committee also 'sets up' a Committee for Party Control. These organs are reproduced, usually in modified form, in the second and third tiers of party organisation, and are examined below. Between 1956 and 1966 the Central Committee also 'created' the Central Committee Bureau of the CPSU for the RSFSR, which consisted of leading party and government officials with special responsibilities in the RSFSR, and was in practice the equivalent of the party Praesidium (as it was then known) in the RSFSR. This Bureau was abolished by the Twenty-Third Congress.

The All-Union Congress is required by the Rules to meet at least once every four years. The scale of representation is determined by the Central Committee—at the Twenty-Second Congress in October 1961 the basis of representation was one voting delegate for every two thousand full members of the party and one delegate without vote for every two thousand probationary or candidate members. (This was a considerably larger basis than ever before and resulted in nearly five thousand delegates.) At the Twenty-Third Congress in March–April 1966 the proportion was one delegate for every two and a half thousand members, and the total number of delegates was about the same. It is clear that a body of this size cannot act as a policy-making body and certainly since 1934, if not before, party congresses have been characterised by a high degree of formality. Their main object is to provide a sounding board, with the widest possible publicity, for the lines of future policy already decided on in advance. The main feature of the Congress is the long report of the Central Committee which is now usually read by its General Secretary. The party Programme and the party Rules must also be laid for approval before the Congress, and minor alterations to the drafts can be (and were in 1961) made in smaller committees of the Congress.

The Central Committee is, under the Rules, in control of all party activity between Congresses. All major decisions of the party are issued under its authority. Among its main responsibilities the Rules list 'selection and distribution of leading cadres', the 'direction' of the work of government departments and voluntary associations and the appointment of editors of central newspapers. As elected at the Twenty-Fifth Party Congress in March 1976, the Central Committee consisted of 287 members and 139 candidate members. The latter do not vote, but it is from their numbers that members who 'drop out' are replaced. (The Rules do not state how the replacements are selected.) Although nominally elected by the Congress, the Central Committee has for many years past followed a fairly fixed pattern: it includes leading party officials, leading officials of the government, and leading representatives of the army, police, education, culture and science. However, even slight variations in its composition, e.g. the extent of army or police representation, usually reflect the influence of the body represented at any particular time.

The Central Committee deliberates in secret, though accounts of some of its deliberations have in recent years often been published. These accounts do not suggest that the Central Committee is much less formal than the Congress but it is likely that more real debate takes place in sessions which are not publicised. The Congress also elects a Central Revision or Auditing Commission, which formally supervises the work of the central apparatus and party finances, but in practice is not of great importance.

The supreme policy-making organ of the party is the Political Bureau, or Politburo, as it is invariably abbreviated. The Politburo was renamed Praesidium at the Nineteenth Congress of the Party in 1952, but the old name was reverted to in April 1966 at the Twenty-Third Party Congress. The Politburo is in theory elected by and responsible to the Central Committee. In practice it is the real centre of power which can, or some members of which can, when required, manipulate the Central Committee. As elected at the Twenty-Fifth Congress, with some changes by death and promotion since then, it consists of fifteen members and six candidate members, who do not vote, except possibly in the absence of a member. It is presided over by the General Secretary, who is often referred to as 'directing' or 'leading' it. Its deliberations are always secret, and no reliable information exists about them.

The Secretariat of the Central Committee (which is charged under the Rules with 'the selection of cadres' and with 'checking on the carrying out of party decisions') has become the most influential organ of the party, and therefore of the country, largely through its control over all appointments, both within the party directly, and in all branches of national life indirectly. It is the general planning staff which provides the policy makers of the Politburo with its basis of expertise. It exercises general supervisory control over the entire party network throughout the country, and hence over the entire life of the nation. It consists of a number of secretaries,[2] headed now by a General Secretary, who was known as First Secretary after the death of Stalin until 1966. Each secretary has responsibility for a group of subjects, or, in the case of the more junior secretaries, for the work of one department of the Secretariat. These subjects are administered through a number of departments and a permanent staff which is estimated at a thousand, or a little more.

The heads of these departments are the most important administrators in the country and to a very large extent act, in respect of the branches which they control, as the planning staff for legislation and administration. The following departments are the most important: Administration of Affairs; Administrative Organs (which deals with the police, the judicial service and the security service); Agriculture; Construction; Culture; Defence Industry; various industrial departments; International (which deals with all foreign policy); Organisational Party Work, which deals with all appointments within the party network and with the selection of candidates to (officially) elective offices and appointments; Chief Political Administration of the Soviet Army and Navy; Propaganda and Agitation; Relations with Communist and Workers' Parties of Socialist Countries; Science and Educational Establishments.*

During the years when the Bureau of the CPSU for the RSFSR was in existence, most of these departments were divided into two, one for the RSFSR and one for the Union Republics, and the departments with responsibility for the RSFSR were grouped under the Bureau of the RSFSR. This practice was abandoned in 1966.

The Committee of Party Control is the supreme disciplinary organ of the party. It is charged with the general supervision of individual party members' conduct and discipline, and their observance of the Party Programme and Rules, and of the party moral code. It is also the supreme appellate instance in all cases of expulsion from the party or of the imposition of disciplinary penalties.

It is obvious that a body of this kind, if independent, could be a great safeguard against acts of injustice committed by the party authorities against members, which it is now freely admitted took place in the past. There was a short time in the early history of the party, from 1920 to 1922, when the Central Control Commission (as it was then called) was elected and given some degree of independence. But for many years past (officially since 1939, in practice since the early twenties) it has been appointed by the central party authorities. It cannot therefore exercise any independent judgement in a case where the individual member comes into conflict with the central authorities or with any act of a local party organ committed with the authority of the central organs. It can only be expected to do justice where a member has been unfairly treated by a local party organ or committee in a manner or in circumstances which do not carry the approval of the central organs.

The central machinery of the party is to a limited extent paralleled in the subordinate party organisations. In the Union republics and in the regions, into which the RSFSR and some other Union republics are subdivided, the supreme authority is respectively the Congress or the Conference. The Congress meets every

*For a complete list, as known in 1976, see Appendix.

five years and the Conference every 2–3 years. (Until the party Rules were amended in 1971, Union Republican Congresses and regional conferences used to meet every four years, except in the Ukraine, Belorussia, Uzbekistan and Kazakhstan, where the Congresses met once in four years.)

It is usual for all these Conferences and Congresses to meet in the months preceding the All-Union Congress and to elect their delegations to it. The Union republics have Central Committees, the regions have committees. All elect in addition a Bureau and secretaries; they are all empowered to set up Secretariats, and usually do. The departmental organisation of the Secretariats varies, but it is broadly similar to that of the All-Union Secretariat. The organisations at this level are responsible for 'directing' the work of the organisations at the next level—the circuit, city and urban and rural district organisations (articles 41 to 47 of the party Rules).

The third-tier organisations are mainly responsible for the 'setting up and confirmation of the primary party organisations and the direction of their activity' (article 50). Their machinery is similar: they have a Conference or general meeting which is required to meet every two years; the Conference elects a committee and the committee elects a Bureau and secretaries, and there is a small permanent office.

The 390,387 primary party organisations (as of January 1976) form the backbone of the party: they are at all events the organisations with which the ordinary member most usually comes into contact and through which the party extends its influence and discipline over him, moulds him and mobilises him for the carrying out of party policy. Primary party organisations are formed in all enterprises and institutions where there are at least three Communists. The policy of the party, in which it has not always succeeded, is to form a primary organisation in every institution. Thus, in the case of the collective farms the reluctance or unsuitability of the collective farmers led to the result that for many years many collective farms were without primary party organisations, which impeded party control. This situation has been largely remedied in the past few years and by April 1965 nearly all collective farms had primaries. Primaries are also set up in all government departments.

The structure of primaries varies according to their size. All have a secretary, but according to the Rules (article 56) full-time paid secretaries should 'as a general practice' only be appointed when the primary exceeds a hundred and fifty members. Where there are more than fifteen members a Bureau is elected annually. The supreme authority within the primary according to the Rules (article 55) is the general meeting, which is required to convene once a month, but the larger primaries are allowed to elect a committee for the direction of activity between general meetings.

The duties of the primaries, which are enumerated at length in the Rules (article 58), fall under three broad heads: first, the recruitment of new members into the party; secondly, educational work both among Communists and non-Communists. So far as Communists are concerned, the primary is made responsible for ensuring their loyalty, the direction of their doctrinal beliefs. In particular its duty is to preserve them from any deviation from the party line, and to ensure that Communists observe the moral code of the party which is now endorsed by the party Programme. This includes such virtues as devotion to the cause of Communism, to the motherland and to the socialist state, hard work, devotion to the public interest, comradely and humane relations with others, honesty and moral integrity and exemplary family life, intolerance of racial prejudice and of the enemies of Communism.

Finally, the primaries are charged with the duty of exercising 'control'[3] over the enterprises in which they are formed. In the case of all enterprises including government departments (since the 24th Congress) this means actual interference in the management in order to ensure its efficiency and enthusiasm. In recent years special commissions have been organised for this purpose in the primaries in order to make their control more effective. This dualism of control—party and management, which runs right through Soviet public and economic life—is one of the most frequent sources of friction. The party organisations are frequently enjoined not to attempt to 'replace' the normal government or economic machinery (see for example article 42 of the Rules). But as they have to take the blame for shortcomings it is only natural that they should at times virtually take over the running of an enterprise. At the 24th Congress of the CPSU in 1971, greater stress than before was laid on the 'Control' function of the primaries, and their area of competence in this respect was extended.

The last four chapters of the party Rules deal with miscellaneous aspects of the party. The party is charged with the general direction of the work of the All-Union Leninist Communist League of Youth (Komsomol). This organisation embraces virtually all youth between the ages of fourteen and twenty-eight, though only a small proportion of Komsomol members ultimately find their way into the party. Two articles deal with the party organisations within the Soviet Army, which are under the direction of the appropriate department of the Central Committee.

Two further articles (67 and 68) deal with the all-important 'party groups'. These temporary groups are set up over and above the existing primaries and committees 'in all Congresses, Conferences, and meetings convened by Soviet, trade union, co-operative and other mass organisations . . . and also in the elected organs of these organisations' where there are more than three Communists. These party groups are under strict orders of submission to the decisions of the appropriate central or territorial party organisations. They form one of the main methods of control over the political activity of the country. The last three articles (69 to 71) deal with party dues which are fixed on a sliding scale, varying with the monthly income of a member—from $\frac{1}{2}\%$ where the monthly income is between 51 and 100 roubles, to 3% where it exceeds 300 roubles.

Party members in the strict sense form about 6% of the total population. But to get a more accurate picture of those who are actually under party discipline it is necessary first to add the older Komsomol members, and secondly to express this total as a percentage of the active population over eighteen alone. This might bring the percentage nearer to 20. Nor does this take account of the numerous non-party 'activists' who co-operate closely with the party, possibly with the intention of joining it. All in all, the party holds under direct discipline a fair proportion of the population. Through its control over the police, legal and government machinery, its indirect discipline extends to every citizen.

Not all party members are equally active. At the lowest end of the scale are those for whom membership is an irksome duty, who joined the party in the interest of their careers. Such members content themselves with mechanical attendance at meetings. At the top of the scale are the well-paid full-time officials. They number perhaps a quarter of a million, but the exact figure has never been published and cannot be estimated with more than approximate accuracy. This forms what is usually known as the 'apparatus' of the party—the network of officials primarily responsible for putting through the policy of the party which emanates from the top. At the apex of this apparatus are the General Secretary of the Central Committee and the Secretariat in Moscow. If, however, all members of party committees and bureaux, together with all secretaries and party group organisers, are taken together, this gives a figure, according to recently published official data, of over 2,600,000, to which must be added the paid officials.

The turnover in the party apparatus is fairly rapid. According to the 1961 Rules tenure of all office in the party was limited—in the Central Committee, for example, one-quarter were required to retire every four years, while lower down the scale a renewal of at least a third was required. (This provision was not systematically observed.) Exception was made in the Rules to provide for the indefinite retention of the services of Communists of exceptional qualities (article 25). However, the system envisaged was not very different from what in fact happened in the past few years. A hard core of important officials remain in office for years—subject to the occasional political eclipses which form the occupational hazard of the member of the apparatus. At the lower levels and in the wider ranges of the party committees turnover is rapid. According to official data published in May 1962, 70·5% of first secretaries were stated to have held their appointments for less than three years, and only 12·8% for over five years. According to information given to the Twenty-Second All-Union Congress in October 1961, in the elections which had just been held in the territorial party organisations, the composition of committees of the second-tier organisations was renewed to the extent of 45%, and that of the third-tier organisations to the extent of 40%.

The Rules (as amended in 1966) include detailed provisions on the conditions of membership. Any Soviet citizen over twenty-three may be a member of the party provided that he recognises the Programme and the Rules, works actively for the construction of Communism, works inside one of the party organisations, carries out the decisions of the party and pays his dues (articles 1 and 4). Candidates under twenty-three years of age may join only through the ranks of the Komsomol. New members, who may be workers, peasants, or members of the intelligentsia, must pass through a probationary stage of one year. At the end of the year the primary decides whether the candidate is worthy of becoming a full

member (articles 4, 14 and 16). A candidate must be recommended
to the primary by three party members of not less than five years'
standing who have known the candidate at his work for at least
a year and the admission of the candidate requires the approval of
both the primary meeting and of the appropriate city or district
party organisation.

Both members and candidates are subject to various disciplinary
actions. For non-payment of dues for three months, without valid
reason, a member is liable to be denounced as having left the party.
This is the only form of resignation provided for by the Rules
(article 8). For other breaches of party discipline both members
and candidate (probationary) members are liable to one of the
following penalties: reprimand or strict reprimand, with or without an entry in the membership card; or expulsion. The question
of expulsion is raised at the general meeting of the primary. A
decision to expel requires the vote of two-thirds of those members
who are present at the meeting (not, be it noted, of *all* members of
the primary), and must be confirmed by the city or urban or rural
district organisation to which the primary is subordinated. The
member if expelled may appeal right up the party hierarchy to the
Central Committee, where the matter is examined by the Committee of Party Control (see p. 66). If the question of expulsion of a
member of a party committee of the second or third tier of organisations (i.e. Union republican Central Committees, regional
committees, city or district committees) arises, it is now, since the
amendment of the Rules in 1966, also decided in the primary, and
approved by the immediately superior city or district committee.
The right of appeal of the member expelled is preserved. A member
or candidate member of the Central Committee, or a member of
the Central Revision Commission, can only be expelled by the All-
Union Congress or by a vote of two-thirds of the members of the
Central Committee (articles 9 to 11). Expulsions from the party
are not infrequent. Over 400,000 were expelled between 1956 and
1964. However, the number is decreasing: some 500,000 had been
expelled between 1951 and 1956. A calling in and exchange of
party cards was ordered by the 24th Congress of the CPSU in 1971.
As stated at the 25th Congress in 1976, 347,000 party cards were
not renewed as the result of this operation.

It may be useful at this point to summarise the main changes in
the structure of the party which were introduced under the direct
influence of Khrushchev, and mainly in early 1963. Very few if any

of these changes (which can be seen in tabular form on Chart Two) survive the fall of Khrushchev. Indeed at the Twenty-Third Congress in 1966 his successor as leader of the party, having already secured the abolition of most of Khrushchev's innovations before the Congress, seemed anxious to break all links with the era of Khrushchev's rule. At least, this seems the most likely explanation for the decision to revert to the old title of General Secretary (used by Stalin after 1922) in place of that of First Secretary, adopted by Khrushchev in 1953; and to rename the Praesidium, as it was known throughout Khrushchev's period of office, by its old name Politburo, which went back to the days of Lenin—and Stalin. Khrushchev's innovations were mainly in three areas of party organisation: in the central apparatus; at the regional and district levels; and in respect of party control.

The first change, dating from 1955, was the creation within the central secretariat of separate departments in the main fields of secretariat activity for the RSFSR and for the Union Republics. In 1956 a separate Bureau of the Central Committee for the RSFSR was created, under which these RSFSR departments of the central secretariat were grouped. In this way the RSFSR Bureau, of which Khrushchev was Chairman, but which included in its directing body the leading party members concerned with the RSFSR, became a kind of Praesidium for the RSFSR, which, it will be recalled, had never previously had a separate party organisation. The RSFSR Bureau, which served Khrushchev well in his struggle against the 'anti-party group', was abolished in 1966.

The remaining innovations date mostly from 1963, and were proposed by him at a Central Committee Plenum in November 1962, and, of course, voted by acclamation unanimously. To continue with changes at the centre, a number of new Commissions and Bureaux were set up. Although these commissions included in their membership the appropriate higher party officials of the relevant departments, and each was headed by a secretary as chairman, they also included other Central Committee members. For example, the Ideological Commission included editors of the important newspapers and similar persons. It would seem that the function of the new commissions was to provide some wider form of party supervision over the all-important subjects of ideology and party appointments that had been possible hitherto.

The new Bureaux were five in number. First there were Bureaux for Industry and Agriculture. These were intended to act as co-ordinating bodies over the republics and over the hierarchy of industrial and agricultural party committees which were created in most of the regions (see below). Then two Bureaux of the Central Committee were set up to act as co-ordinating offices for two important branches of national production—one for (Heavy) Industry and Construction, and another for the Chemical and Light Industries. Again, it may be assumed that these Bureaux were designed to act as a yet higher level instance of direction over the day-to-day high-level direction over the Ministries exercised by the normal production branch departments which still continued to exist within the Secretariat.

Finally, the Central Asian Bureau was set up: its membership included the first secretaries of the four Central Asian Republics. (Its chairman was a Russian party official from Moscow.) The Central Asian Bureau seemed to exercise direct authority over the Central Asian CNE, cutting out the republican Councils of Ministers. This type of direct party intervention from the centre was a revival of a method of party administration which fell into disuse after 1953.

A really novel departure was the setting up of the Committee of Party and State Control of the Central Committee of the CPSU and of the Council of Ministers of the USSR. This was a nation-wide joint party-state organ with very extensive powers of control, and highly centralised in structure (see chapter 8 for further details). It was headed by a secretary of the party (at all levels) and, so far as its function in relation to the party was concerned, took over the disciplinary duties of the old Party Control Committee. The latter was renamed the Party Commission attached to the Central Committee of the CPSU and its functions restricted to the hearing of appeals by party members against expulsion and other party penalties.

The main change in the republican party organisations was the setting up in each of a Praesidium (in place of a Bureau), of which the First Secretary was chairman. The departments of the republican Central Committees were made either directly subordinate to the Praesidium, e.g. the departments of administrative (including police, law and security) organs; or to one or other of two new Bureaux—for industry and for agriculture. Thus, each of these new Bureaux was in charge of the appropriate industrial or agricultural departments (which varied in stucture in different republics) and in addition had its own separate departments for Party Organs and for Ideology. The newly constituted Praesidia were designed to act as co-ordinating bodies for what might otherwise be a somewhat diffuse and disjointed machine.

The greatest changes were effected lower down the hierarchy—in the regions and districts. The majority of the regional committees (which, for party purposes, include ASSR and autonomous regional committees) were split into two—one for industry and one for agriculture, each headed by a first secretary. In the RSFSR, for example, forty-five out of seventy-eight regional and area party committees were so divided. (In the country as a whole there were in June 1963 218 area and regional party committees, as compared with 153 on 1 October 1961.) Each (functional) regional committee had four secretaries—the third and fourth were respectively chairmen of the ideological department and of the local party-state control committee. Apart from the ideological department, each of the two committees had departments for party organs and for the branches of industry or agriculture appropriate to the individual region. But only the industrial regional committee had an administrative organs department—the department which deals with police and legal matters.

If the number of regional committees was thus somewhat increased, the number of committees lower down the scale was drastically reduced. In general, the direct supervision of the industrial primary party organisations was left in the hands of the existing city committees and city municipal (district) committees. All that happened mostly was that these were re-grouped. But in some cases new committees were created within the new 'zonal industrial production directorates', which were set up as the administrative organs for industry within predominantly agricultural areas. But the total number was almost the same—950 in all in 1963 as against 945 in October 1961.

The rural district committees, on the other hand, were abolished. Their place, as the main party organ for the supervision over primary party organisations in the collective and state farms, was taken by the new party committees which were set up inside the 'Kolkhoz-sovkhoz territorial production administrations' (for these see chapter 6). The total number of these new party committees was about 1,500 in 1963 as compared with 3,200 rural district party committees in October 1961.

Three main reasons were advanced for these drastic changes in the party structure. First, the need to reduce the total number of party officials; secondly, the need to provide for greater specialisation in the supervisory functions of the party; and thirdly, the desire to eliminate conflict of responsibilities between party functionaries and those responsible for administering industry and agriculture.

There was probably a good deal of truth so far as the aims expressed by Khrushchev were concerned. He deserves some credit for making a new and valiant attempt to achieve two things. First, to eliminate the traditional friction between the party and the government machine by some kind of fusion between the two. And secondly, by dividing the responsibility of the powerful First Secretary of the region into two, to reduce somewhat the overwhelming power which these officials had accumulated: obviously neither of two parallel secretaries was going to be so powerful as the one single one whom they replaced. On the other hand, there is no doubt that these measures proved very unpopular with the party apparatus—not least the abolition of the rural district secretaries, thousands of whom were thrown out of jobs. Critics of the reforms, who became as vocal in their criticism of them after Khrushchev's fall as they had been enthusiastic for them while he was in power, were able to point with justification to the confusion and lack of co-ordination which additional complexities of organisational structure had brought in their train.

None of the changes enumerated above has survived the fall of Khrushchev. The divided regions were reunited and the abolished district committees restored by November 1964. The Party State Control Committee was reduced to a purely state organ, with no party functions, in 1965: its party functions (which incidentally the party had successfully prevented from exercising) were once again restored to the Committee of Party Control of the Central Committee. The RSFSR Bureau was abolished at the Twenty-Third Congress in April 1966. The other innovations at the centre have not been expressly repealed, but the evidence suggests that none of the new commissions or bureaux remains in being.

The question of the relation of party to state, indeed of party to state and society, lies at the core of all Soviet government and will be examined from different aspects in the chapters which follow.

Certain general features of the relationship should however be noted at the outset.

In the first place the party enjoys, and always has enjoyed, in practice if not in official avowal, a greater prestige than any other section of the apparatus of power. It is the party which, in official doctrine, stood for the best and the most politically conscious citizens from among the historically predestined ruling class, the proletariat. As time has proceeded, the conception of the social predominance of the proletariat gave way to that of the 'toilers' as a whole: the workers, the peasants and the intellectuals. Logically enough, since all 'exploiters' are stated to have been eliminated as far back as in the period of collectivisation of the peasants, the Programme of the party adopted in October 1961 (to replace the earlier Programme which dated from 1919) now states that the party is the vanguard of the entire nation. It still remains the élite believed officially to be endowed with an inherent right to guide and direct—even if it can no longer invoke the authority of Marx to the same extent as it could while the party remained identified with the proletariat.

In practice this means, in the first place, that it is from the party and from the party alone that all policy emanates at all levels. At the top, this policy will emanate from the Praesidium, often enunciated in directives issued in the joint names of the Council of Ministers and of the Central Committee of the CPSU. But, as will be seen in the following chapters, this predominance of the party as sole policy maker is to be found at all levels—in the network of Soviets, for example, in the legal machinery, or in the functioning of industry—though it is the case that since the new collective leadership has taken over the government, leaders have been able to assert a greater degree of independence in matters concerning industry and planning.

This predominance of the party at all levels is, to al arge extent, achieved by the fact that suitable party members are placed in the right position—from the top, say, in the Council of Ministers, where the leading ministers are at the same time leading party members, to the village Soviet, where the real authority will be found to be in the hands of certain leading Communist members of its executive committee. It is for this reason that the placing of its members in positions throughout the country has always been a matter of vital concern to the party—to quote Stalin, 'Cadres decide everything'. But in addition the party disposes of a national network of committees at all territorial levels, and in virtually all institutions in the form of a primary party organisation. The authority of these party committees, or more usually of their secretaries, is, on paper, usually advisory and exhortatory. They are in practice more often than not put in a position of greater authority than that, if only because it is to them that one has to look in the Soviet Union for sole guidance in expounding policy, the party line. It is here also that the greater prestige enjoyed by the party comes into play, the realisation that the all-important voice of Moscow is at the end of the telephone at the local party secretary's elbow. Moreover, it is often the party and the party alone that in practice can 'get things done'.

Signs appeared in the course of 1965 that yet another serious attempt was being made to eliminate the eternal friction between the party officials and the technical experts or soviet administrators. The party was once again being exhorted by the Central Committee to confine its activities to the indoctrination and selection of cadres, and to avoid trying to replace the technician or the administrator. Only time can show whether this new campaign will produce more concrete results in redefining the respective areas of the dual apparatus than have resulted from such campaigns in the past.

This great authority of the party in relation to the vast and complicated state and social machinery which will be described below can, however, only be achieved if the party speaks in one voice, if it is disciplined and united. The experience of the early years of the Soviet regime showed how easily, in the absence of machinery for maintaining discipline over members, breakaways could take place, even if Communists were in local control. The lessons have never been forgotten, and the party, throughout all its strains and vicissitudes, has remained a centralised, disciplined body in which debate is inhibited and in which policy is handed down from above.

This is not to say that those at the top who, with the aid of the central apparatus, formulate policy and transmit its demands, always ignore opinion in the party or in the country as a whole. This has indeed often happened in the past—for much of Stalin's reign, for example. It is not the case now. In many instances the party leaders use all means at their disposal to ascertain opinion at all levels before embarking on a new policy. In general, the initiative for ascertaining opinion must come from the top—years of discipline and severe repression have discouraged any free pressure of opinion from below. Moreover, the party is naturally suspicious of the formation of anything in the nature of lobbies or pressure groups which aim at furthering some interest or point of view. But the party does seek and invite opinion on its own initiative. It can, of course, ignore this opinion—though it probably does so less now than in many periods in the past. There is doctrinal justification for this in the views of Lenin—the function of the 'vanguard' is to lead, not yield to 'spontaneity'. But there are many occasions when the results of a free debate, or group discussions organised by the Central Committee with interested experts, can be seen to have had their effect on a newly produced policy in the form of modifications. At lower levels, where discussion centres on the practical implementation of policy and not on the policy itself, debate is certainly freer today than it was in Stalin's day.

However, in two respects the formulation of the policy of the party and the enforcement of that policy on the state machine has remained unchanged since the early years of Soviet power. In the first place, all initiative comes from above, from the leaders, and in the last resort from one leader, the General Secretary. He may and no doubt often does consult his colleagues. He needs and uses the expert advice tendered by his apparatus. But in the last resort he is the virtual master of appointments, he is the man who can 'hire and fire', and he is therefore the man who can nearly always make his own views prevail against any opposition.

Secondly and for the same reason, the influence which party opinion can exercise on policy is strictly limited. It may, on occasions, be sufficiently taken into account to lead to a certain policy being adopted and it may lead to modification of a policy proposed. But, in the last resort, it is the party apparatus, and this means the party leaders and particularly the General Secretary, the master of the apparatus, who holds the whip hand. The apparatus can silence unwelcome criticism, it can curtail debate, and it can sidestep responsible opinion, because in the last resort the livelihood and position of every critic and of everyone who voices his opinion depends upon it. The extent to which it uses this vast power, which has sometimes been described as 'totalitarian', varies at different periods. It depends on a whole host of imponderable factors—among others on the personalities involved and the degree of confidence which the leaders may feel at any time in the continued docility of the population. It is still the determining feature of the nature of power which the party can and does wield.

1. The distinction between 'organ' and 'organisation' in this context is broadly the distinction between the permanent party officials and Committees and the membership as a whole.

2. Twelve in January 1977, of whom five are full members and one a candidate member of the Politburo.

3. The word 'control' in Russian strictly means 'supervision'. In practice 'supervision' by the party very often tends to become 'control' in the English sense.

4

THE CONSTITUTIONAL STRUCTURE

In 1970 the constitution in force was still the one that had been adopted on 5 December 1936. It had been frequently amended in the course of thirty-two years, but its main features remained substantially unaltered.

It will be recalled that the adoption of a new Constitution, which coincided with the worst period of nation-wide purges and repressions, was a political act of considerable importance, probably intended by Stalin as a sop to the opposition until such time as he could destroy it. Certainly, every effort was made to create the appearance of a whole nation dedicated, under the leadership of Stalin and the party, to the principles of democracy. When the changes in the Constitution were first suggested in February 1935 (in the Plenum of the Central Committee of the Party) they were stated to be directed towards 'further democratisation of the electoral system' and towards making the Constitution correspond to the new class relations brought about by the defeat of the class enemy (the *kulaks*) in the villages; and by the establishment of socialist ownership of industry and collective farming as the basis of Soviet society. By June 1936 the draft was completed by the commission which had been set up to prepare it. This commission included leading oppositionists who were to be shot shortly afterwards, and the work of drafting fell largely to the leading former 'right' oppositionist, Bukharin. In addition to the changes suggested in February 1935, the draft also contained a new chapter on the rights and duties of citizens.

After an extensively publicised and organised nation-wide discussion, the draft was finally unanimously approved, on Stalin's proposal, by the Extraordinary Eighth All-Union Congress of Soviets. The discussion, either at the numerous public meetings or in the Congress, had little effect on the draft, to which very few amendments, and none of real substance, were made. The adoption of the Constitution was made the occasion not only for further adulation of Stalin (an exercise for which any pretext sufficed at that period in the USSR) but also for a demonstration of the free and democratic nature of the Soviet regime both at home and abroad. The widespread approval of the draft was invoked as evidence of the legitimacy of the regime. The one-party system, according to Stalin, ensured democracy for the working people which in the Soviet Union now meant democracy for all. The Soviet Constitution was thus 'the only thoroughly democratic constitution in the world', and would give 'moral assistance and real support to all those who are today fighting fascist barbarism'. If any of his listeners reflected that at that very moment the security police were busily rounding up tens if not hundreds of thousands of victims for the firing squad or concentration camp, they prudently kept their peace.

The Constitution (or Fundamental Law) of 1936 (as amended to date) of the Union of Soviet Socialist Republics contains 146 articles grouped into thirteen chapters. Chs. III to VIII, which deal with legislative and administrative organs at All-Union, republican and local level, will be discussed in chapters 6 and 7 below. Ch. IX, which deals with the courts and the procurators, and ch. XI, which deals with the electoral system, are discussed respectively in chapters 8 and 5 below.

The first chapter of the Constitution deals with social structure, and consists of twelve articles. These articles recite the claim that the USSR is a socialist state in which all power is vested in the toilers of the towns and villages (articles 1–3). The economic base of the state is socialist ownership of the means of production, which takes the form either of national or state ownership or of co-operative collective ownership (articles 4 and 5). State property includes land and ores, factories, mines, all forms of transport and communications, banks and state farms. In the collective farms the land is secured in perpetuity for exploitation by the toiling peasants. The remaining property of the collective farm is owned co-operatively, save that each family is allowed for its private use a small plot of land and enjoys the ownership of the stock which it is permitted to hold on this plot—including some poultry and cattle within strictly prescribed limits (articles 6–8). The Constitution also permits private farming based on personal labour and excluding exploitation, although this form of land holding has been virtually obsolete for some years. The right to personal property, consisting of savings, a dwelling house and household articles and other articles for personal use, as well as the right of inheritance, are preserved. At the same time the duty of each able-bodied citizen to work for the common benefit is proclaimed (articles 9–12).

The second chapter of the Constitution is the one in which the federal structure of the USSR is enacted. Under article 13 the USSR is described as a state 'founded on the basis of the voluntary union' of fifteen equal Soviet Socialist Republics. These are the Russian Soviet Federal Socialist Republic (RSFSR); and the Ukrainian, Belorussian, Uzbek, Kazakh, Georgian, Armenian, Azerbaidjanian, Lithuanian, Moldavian, Latvian, Kirgiz, Tadjik, Turkmen and Estonian Soviet Socialist Republics. The extent to which the agreement for union in 1922 of the original members—the Russian, Ukrainian, Belorussian and Transcaucasian republics—can be said to have been 'voluntary' has already been discussed. In the case of some of the others, the Lithuanian, Latvian and Estonian republics for example, incorporation took place under threat of military force, and the resistance of the local populations was put down by ruthless police measures. However, it must be recalled that the fundamental principle of Soviet political doctrine, which owes its origin to Lenin, is that the Communist Party has the unquestionable right as 'vanguard' to decide the destinies of a people, and therefore the adherence to the Soviet Union of the small local parties in these three and in other republics, even in the teeth of opposition from the majority of the population, can in Communist terminology be described as 'voluntary'. Similarly, the resistance of the populations (which in some cases continued for years after the end of the Second World War) can be described as 'counter-revolution'.

A glance at the map will show that each of these republics borders on foreign territory, and indeed in Soviet theory no territory which does not border on foreign territory can acquire the status of a Union republic. This is because of the right to secede, which is guaranteed by article 17 to each Union republic, and which is regarded by Soviet writers as the most important single characteristic of Soviet federalism. It is in some ways a strange provision, which is not to be found in other federal constitutions —the American civil war, for example, was fought over this very issue. Moreover, in Soviet conditions the right is purely theoretical. It has been openly recognised since the early twenties that the exercise of the right to secede would be (in Stalin's words) 'profoundly counter-revolutionary', and would justify the use of force to prevent it.

Apart from the right of secession, the Constitution depicts a structure which is both much more closely-knit and much more centrifugal than is usually the case in federations. Thus, on the one hand, the laws of the Union are of equal validity in every republic, and prevail, in the event of a discrepancy, over republican laws (articles 19 and 20); the Praesidium of the All-Union Supreme Soviet has the power to set aside decrees and decisions of the Councils of Ministers of the Union republics in the event of their being 'inconsistent with the law' (article 49(f)); and the All-Union Council of Ministers can issue decrees and decisions which are binding throughout the territory of the USSR (article 67). In spite however of the fact that conduct of foreign relations is reserved to the Union, an amendment was adopted in 1944 entitling each republic to enter into direct diplomatic relations and conclude treaties with foreign governments, and to maintain its own republican military force (articles 18a and 18b). This amendment was adopted in order to enable Belorussia and the Ukraine to be separately represented in the United Nations, thus giving the USSR three votes, and has not otherwise had much practical effect. The Soviet Army in particular has remained centralised under All-Union control.

The sovereignty of each Union republic is only limited (by article 15) in the spheres which are enumerated in article 14. This article lists twenty-four spheres in which the Union enjoys the exclusive right of competence. This list may be divided into three main heads: external political matters, internal political matters and internal economic matters. Under the first head fall: international representation, the conclusion, ratification and denunciation of treaties; war and peace; the admission of new Union republics; approval of the alteration of boundaries between republics; approval of the formation of new autonomous republics and autonomous regions (see chapter 5) within the territory of the republics; defence, including the 'determination of directing principles governing' the organisation of the military formations of the Union republics; and foreign trade. The internal political powers include 'control over the observance of the Constitution of the USSR and ensuring conformity of the constitutions of the Union republics with the Constitution of the USSR' (article 14(d)); state security; establishing the 'basic principles' governing education and public health; laying down the 'bases' of civil, family, criminal and procedural legislation, legislation on nationality, and on the legal rights of foreigners, and declaring amnesties. The third heading, which contains the most far-reaching powers, includes the power to lay down the national All-Union economic plan; the administration of banks and of industrial and agricultural enterprises 'of All-Union significance'; transport and communications 'of All-Union significance'; the money, tax and credit system; state insurance; loans, establishing the 'basic principles' of land usage and of the exploitation of natural resources; economic statistics; labour legislation. Most important of all perhaps is article 14(k): 'Approval of the consolidated state budget of the USSR and of the report on its fulfilment; determination of the taxes and revenues which go to the Union, the republican and local budgets'—in other words, the power of complete control over the revenue and expenditure of the Union republics.

The extensive nature of the Union powers is obvious enough and for many years, certainly during the last twenty years of Stalin's strictly centralised control, the independent powers of the republics were so limited as to be virtually non-existent. This has certainly changed to some extent, as will be evident when the present powers of the republics are discussed (see chapter 7). Yet the limited powers now enjoyed by the republican governments are only to a slight extent the result of actual constitutional amendments. In practice the powers which they at any one period are allowed to enjoy depend on the decision of the Union government. The quotations from the relevant articles of the Constitution cited above gives some indication of the extensive powers which exist even on paper, if the Union government chooses to exercise them. What is even more striking, or should be to anyone familiar with the nature of constitutional law, is the abundance of widely drafted phrases which could give rise to a host of legitimately varying interpretations—'basic principles', or 'of All-Union significance', for example. It is, however, a cardinal feature

of Soviet constitutional law and practice that they do not provide
the republican governments with any method of challenging an
All-Union law on the grounds that it conflicts with the legal
autonomy left by the terms of the Constitution to the sphere of
republican action; or on the grounds that it is in the extent of its
purported application in excess of the powers assigned to the
Union. True, article 49(e) requires the Praesidium of the (All-
Union) Supreme Soviet to hold a referendum on the demand of a
Union republic. But this procedure has never been put into effect,
and it is unlikely, so long as all policy is controlled by a highly
centralised party, that it would be. The only remaining relevant
provision of the Constitution is article 49(f) (already referred to)
which empowers the Praesidium of the Supreme Soviet to set aside
a decree of a republican Council of Ministers. The procurators,
the main guardians of legality, who are officials appointed by the
Supreme Soviet, have no power to interfere with acts of the
Supreme Soviet, and are in any case not controlled by the republican authorities. Finally, the Supreme Court of the Union has
certain powers to deal with conflicts of judicial acts under a
Statute of 12 February 1957. Thus it is empowered to deal with
conflicts between several republican Supreme Courts; and it can
deal with complaints presented by the President of the All-Union
Supreme Court or by the Procurator General of the Union to the
effect that the act of a republican Supreme Court either violates
All-Union law, or conflicts with the interests of other republics.
But these provisions do not relate to legislative acts; and are in any
case only available to the Union for use against the republics, and
not the other way round.

Thus, the extent of competence enjoyed by the republics at any
time can ultimately only depend on the will of the Union to allow
them independence of action in this sphere or that. This is not to
say that the views of the republics are ignored—they participate,
for example, extensively in the preparation of their own budgets
(see chapter 7) and they are represented both in the All-Union
Supreme Soviet (in the Council of Nationalities) and in the All-
Union Council of Ministers (see chapter 6). But the decision rests
with the All-Union authorities. This state of affairs renders rather
academic the provision of article 15 of the Constitution that the
republics are sovereign except as limited by article 14 and that the
'USSR safeguards the sovereign rights of the Union republics',
since there is no means of enforcing this duty laid upon the Union.

This has led some students of Soviet constitutional law to doubt whether the USSR can properly be described as a federation at all; and to suggest that in reality the USSR is a unitary state with a measure of administrative devolution.

However, two features seem to render this kind of discussion of Soviet federalism rather unrealistic. First, there is the question of the party. As already shown above, the party, both in theory and in practice, is the real source of all legislative policy and the controlling factor behind the formal organs described in the Constitution. But the party is centralised and has from the outset, certainly since 1903, repudiated the federal principle. The party organisations of the Union republics are not national parties, but branches of the single unitary Communist Party of the Soviet Union. Hence, whatever the constitutional provisions in force may be at any time, the ultimate deciding factor on all matters of policy will be the party, and this by its very nature must mean in practice the central supreme party organs at the top in Moscow, if not the supreme leader or leaders. This factor both acts as a restraint on decentralisation and ensures that when it does take place it is restricted to the administrative and does not extend to the decision-making sphere.

Secondly, the geographical and economic facts of the Soviet Union alone are sufficient to make the existing division into republics quite inappropriate for a national industrial policy. As is evident both from the map and from the details which will be found below (see chapter 5) the RSFSR and the Ukraine between them contain the overwhelming bulk of the nation's industrial wealth. Moreover in population and in the number of its cities the RSFSR is important out of all proportion in relation to all the other republics, even including the Ukraine. These facts of population and economic geography are naturally of particular importance in a country where the national planning of all industry has played so large a part since 1929. Their importance indeed is such that it has meant in practice that the republics have often been of little relevance where industrial regionalisation has been concerned. Until some years after Stalin's death the republican pattern was virtually ignored so far as industry was concerned by a system of almost complete centralisation of control. In 1957 a very considerable decentralisation of control over industry was embarked upon and some 105 economic regions were created. During the few years of the existence of this system (it lasted from 1957 until

1965) the number of regions was considerably reduced. Even so, the pattern of the regionalisation of industry which the new system was based on, followed criteria, both political and economic, to which the administrative framework of fifteen Union republics was largely irrelevant (see chapter 6).

The origin of the federal, or quasi-federal, pattern of the USSR is thus not to be found in any economic or political reality. It is in fact more a consequence of the doctrine of nationalities developed and accepted by Lenin and his successors. For Marx himself nationalism remained a retrograde phenomenon, inconsistent with socialism, and the internationalism of the proletariat. Lenin, with more of an eye than Marx on the technique of making revolution, realised the explosive force which nationalism offered against the imperialist and colonialist powers, especially within the Russian Empire. He therefore insisted, in face of much opposition from his more orthodox colleagues, on incorporating into Bolshevik doctrine nationalist claims, including the right of free secession for all the nationalities of the Russian Empire. What Lenin's colleagues did not perhaps realise is the extent to which in Lenin's view the concept of nationalism was flexible and dependent on the particular situation. Thus nationalism was viewed as a progressive force in Russia before 1917 because it could serve to break up the Russian Empire: yet by the early twenties it was already regarded as a retrograde force in the case of those portions of the former Russian Empire which had been reintegrated into the new Soviet state. Similarly, nationalism remained a 'progressive force' so far as, for example, India and other colonial territories were concerned.

Broadly, this 'dialectical' view of nationalism remains the official Sovet doctrine. The new Programme which the party adopted in October 1961 strongly condemns all forms of political nationalism both among the nations composing the Soviet Union and within the nations composing the Soviet block of states—among the latter it is described as the chief instrument 'used by international reaction . . . against the unity of the socialist countries'. But in those countries where the influence of the imperialists persists it is 'an important factor in the progressive development of society'.

So far as internal policy is concerned, Soviet treatment of the many non-Russian nationalities, which compose the population of the Soviet Union, can be divided into three phases. Lenin's policy may be summarised as extensive concessions in matters of culture, minor concessions in the matter of self government in the case of the Union republics and the autonomous republics and no concessions at all in the matter of party organisation. Stalin's policy was in theory a continuation of Lenin's and in practice one of increasing emphasis on the predominance of the Great Russian language and culture. During his reign extensive repressions took place not only against Communists within the ethnic minorities who showed signs of attempting to promote national forms of Communism (in this he would have had Lenin's full support) but also against national culture in general and against several entire such nations in particular. The denial of cultural and language rights and the other repressive measures were in part attributable not so much to anything which can be described as a nationalities 'policy', as to the general terror and violence which Stalin employed against Russians and non-Russians alike. But there was an element of theory involved to the extent that the ethnic minorities were compelled to accept their subjection to Russian rule in the past as an historically progressive fact, and to acknowledge the Great Russians as 'Elder brothers'.

Nationalities policy since Stalin's death has undergone modification in the general direction of greater tolerance which characterises present-day policy when compared with that of Stalin. However, few significant concessions have been made to ethnic minorities even in matters of language and culture and the suspicion of nationalism as a potentially disruptive force is as strong as ever it was. In general, in so far as members of the ethnic minorities are concerned, the Soviet regime places no obstacles in the way of their advancement (at any rate not officially—there are signs of unofficial discrimination, especially in the case of Jews) provided they are ready to conform in all respects to overall Soviet policy. This, after all, is little different from the case of every Soviet citizen, Russian or non-Russian. But the non-Russian national faces a particular problem because of the highly centralised nature of the Soviet state with its great concentration of Russian (or Russian and Ukrainian) technical and administrative talent and with an administration necessarily conducted in Russian. In order to succeed in such a system some degree of assimilation, especially in the matter of language, is forced upon the non-Russian. This process of assimilation has been much facilitated by the extensive movements of population which have in many parts of the Soviet Union put an end to the numerical domination of one national minority—the Kazakhs, for example, already form a minority of the population in Kazakhstan. The new Programme welcomes the trend towards assimilation of non-Russians, and looks forward to the time when a 'new stage in the development of national relations in the USSR' will be reached and 'complete unity' eventually achieved. It also asserts that 'an international culture common to all the Soviet nations is developing' and that the Russian language has become the 'common medium of intercourse'. In short, there is no doubt that the aim of the present rulers of the USSR is to move away from federalism towards greater unity, and to sweep away national distinctions by total assimilation. Whether they will succeed without violent administrative measures, or even with them, is another matter.

However, the Constitution still asserts (article 123) the equality of all citizens irrespective of race or nationality in all spheres of 'economic, government, cultural and public and political life', and provides for repression by the criminal law of all forms of 'direct or indirect' national or racial discrimination. The value of this provision of the Constitution must be judged in the general light of the value of ch. X as a whole, of which this article forms a part. It may however be observed that the provisions of this article did not prevent the wholesale deportations during the war, under conditions which caused enormous casualties, of no less than seven nationalities, which were dispersed in Siberia and Central Asia. The survivors of five of the seven were 'rehabilitated' in 1956, the charges of disloyalty against them admitted to be trumped up, and they were allowed to return to their homes, but the survivors of two other national groups—the Volga Germans and the Crimean Tartars—still remain in their exile. Nearly a million people in all were affected.

Ch. X of the Constitution is headed 'The Basic Rights and Duties of Citizens', and consists of sixteen articles. The appearance of this chapter in the draft in 1936 came as a surprise to some, since no reference had been made to it in the Central Committee Plenum in February 1935 when directions were issued on the subjects to be covered by the draft of the new Constitution. The rights ostensibly guaranteed in this chapter seemed to have aroused some apprehensions (or hopes) among party members that greater tolerance was envisaged in the future towards opinion other than official opinion. At any rate the party newspaper *Pravda* hastened to reassure its readers (on 22 June 1936) that 'we shall not give a scrap of paper nor an inch of space for those who think differently' from the party. Yet, even without this reassurance, a careful reading of the draft (which was enacted without any serious amendment) should have convinced any reader that the rights guaranteed were circumscribed in such a way as not to impair the dominant position of the party—as indeed was pointed out by Stalin in his speech when the Constitution was adopted.

Articles 118 to 122 establish the economic rights of the citizen. These are naturally given pride of place, because of the insistence of Marx, and Lenin after him, that the civil freedoms guaranteed by the constitutional law of bourgeois societies are valueless in the absence of a guarantee to all of a sufficient economic independence to make their enjoyment a reality. The five economic rights guaranteed by these articles are: the right to employment, the right to leisure, the right to support in old age and in sickness, the right to education and equality of rights for women. These guarantees have been (and are) honoured to a varying extent at different periods of Soviet history, depending on the policy of the rulers and on economic and other conditions at any particular time. But it may be observed that, so far as the individual is concerned, the Constitution affords him no means of enforcing these rights, by action in the courts, for example, or otherwise. They are thus more in the nature of declarations of policy and indeed the form in which they are cast makes this clear. For in each case the guarantee of the particular right is followed by a paragraph of explanation of the way in which this right is 'assured'. Thus the right to employment is 'assured' by the socialist system of economic organisation, the growth of productivity and the elimination of crises and of unemployment. Similarly, the right to security in sickness and old age is 'assured' by the widespread development of social insurance of 'workers and employees at state expense'. In practice, however, it cannot be assured by these means to all 'citizens of the USSR', as article 120 claims, since the peasants, who still form nearly half of the labour force, are not included in the category of 'workers and employees' and are therefore not normally covered by social insurance. Yet this does not, in Soviet law, give the collective farm peasant (the peasant on the state farm is an 'employee') a right of action in the courts to enforce his 'right' as a citizen under article 120. These examples could be multiplied without end. There is however little point in doing so, because this would be to ignore the essentially declaratory nature of all these 'guarantees'.

Civil rights and freedoms are covered by articles 124 to 128. Separation of church and state and church and school are declared in the interest of ensuring 'freedom of conscience'. The same article (article 124) also recognises freedom of religious worship and freedom of anti-religious propaganda—a formulation which was intended to exclude freedom of religious instruction and propaganda. (Until 18 May 1929 freedom of both religious and anti-religious propaganda was guaranteed in the individual constitutions of all the republics.) The next article guarantees to all citizens of the USSR freedom of speech, freedom of the press, freedom of association and meetings, and freedom of street processions and demonstrations. The guarantee is given 'in accordance with the interests of the toilers' and 'with the aim of strengthening socialist order'. Since in prevalent Soviet practice no criticism of party policy could possibly be regarded as 'strengthening the socialist order' these words are already a wide limitation. The guarantee is further limited by an assertion that these rights are 'assured' by the fact that 'the toilers' are supplied with printing presses, papers, public buildings and other material conditions necessary for the enjoyment of the guaranteed rights. If any 'toilers' with views unacceptable to the party leaders were to claim under this article the right to paper and printing facilities, their claim could easily be met by the retort that this was not in the interest of 'strengthening the socialist order'—even if no worse consequences were to follow such an unlikely event.

Article 126, which guarantees the right of citizens to unite in voluntary associations, trade unions, co-operatives, cultural, sporting and scientific societies and the like, is mainly remarkable for its open mention of the Communist Party. It was the first time that the party had been mentioned in the Constitution—neither the RSFSR Constitution of 1918 nor the first USSR Constitution of 1924 had referred to its existence. 'The most active and conscious citizens from the ranks of the working class, the toiling peasants and the toiling intelligentsia', says article 136, 'voluntarily unite in the Communist Party of the Soviet Union, which is the vanguard of the toilers in their struggle for the construction of

Communism, and which represents the directing core of all organisations of the toilers, both voluntary and state.' (This is the text currently in force: in 1936 it was slightly different because the task then was considered to be the strengthening and development of socialism as a preliminary stage to Communism.) Finally, two articles (127 and 128) guarantee freedom of person, the inviolability of domicile and secrecy of correspondence.

Foreign citizens who are persecuted for defending the interests of the workers, for scientific activity or for national liberation struggle, are offered asylum by article 129. The remaining four articles of this chapter set out the duties of the citizen: these are the duty to observe the Constitution, the laws and the rules of socialist communal life; the duty to guard and respect public property; the duty to serve with the armed forces; and the duty to defend and preserve the security of his country.

It was already observed in discussing the rights of the Union republics under the Constitution that it was not open to a republic to question in the courts an All-Union law which may override its constitutional rights. The individual citizen is in the same position. Neither the Constitution itself nor Soviet legal practice knows anything of the system of judicial review, or review by the courts of a law in order to determine whether or not it conflicts with the Constitution. There is therefore no judicial means by which the citizen can demand enforcement of the rights conferred upon him by the Constitution; nor any judicial means by which the validity of any law can be challenged. There is to be sure the administrative supervision of legality by the Procurators which is dealt with later (see chapter 8) and it is open to an aggrieved citizen to appeal to the Procurators. There are also other administrative avenues of appeal and complaints. These methods no doubt often provide redress in cases where no questions of policy are involved. They are however quite useless when the administration itself has decided upon a course of arbitrary conduct. The innumerable violations of legality—illegal arrests, torture, execution and exile—which went on for many years under Stalin, and which have been freely admitted and condemned by his successors, took place at a time when the present Constitution was already in force.

Aside from the case of the violation of the constitutional right of the individual, legislation which is in direct conflict with the Constitution is by no means infrequent. In many cases, probably in most cases, the discrepancy is eventually put right by an amendment of the Constitution—though it should be noted that the 'unconstitutional' law or decree is fully valid before the consequential amendment takes place. There are known cases where no such amendment is even considered necessary. A common example is a decree withdrawing the land held by a collective farm—where this is necessary for a public purpose, such as the construction of a railway. However great the necessity, such a decree is in fact a violation of article 8 of the Constitution which guarantees the use of their land 'in perpetuity' to collective farms. As will be seen below (chapter 6) amendment of the Constitution is regularly and frequently necessitated whenever a change is made in the numbers and titles of ministries. The process of amendment is the subject of ch. XIII, which consists of one article (146). This requires a majority of at least two-thirds of the votes in each of the two Chambers of the Supreme Soviet. Since this body has never on a single occasion, since it first met in 1937, been recorded as voting otherwise than by complete unanimity, this requirement has never given rise to any practical difficulty. To complete the account of those parts of the Constitution of which the description is not postponed, it only remains to mention ch. XII, which consists of three articles (143–5) setting out the national emblem and flag, and fixing Moscow as the capital.

Since the Constitution is in many respects more honoured in the breach than in the observance, the question may well be asked: what purpose does it serve? It is, of course, in the first place a useful shop-window, both at home and abroad. A revolutionary state, with a mission of expanding its influence, needs all the instruments of propaganda that it can muster. The formulae of the Constitution, even if they are only empty shells, are often drafted with this propaganda object well in mind. Secondly, the Constitution provides a framework, a hierarchy of Soviets and administrative and judicial organs, without which no large state can exist. When required, which seems to be quite often in practice, the administrative arm, through the machinery of the party, can effect the result it wishes in spite of any inconvenient provision in the Constitution. But even if the law is often violated it is none the less convenient to know what the law is.

Thirdly, it may be that the Constitution should be regarded as an ideal towards which Soviet society is evolving. This view is strictly at variance with theory—a Constitution, so doctrine asserts, is the picture of what actually is, here and now: the aim and ideals for the future should be set out in a Programme. Nevertheless, the Constitution exists on paper and it is well realised by the Soviet rulers that it has been much violated in past years. These violations are frequently condemned and the need for conformity to the law frequently stressed. Since conformity to the law necessarily also means conformity to the Constitution, it follows that at any time when a genuine effort is made to practise greater respect for the law, the provisions of the Constitution will necessarily be looked to as a model to which law and practice should conform.

It is therefore of some interest that in the course of 1962 projects were set afoot for drafting a new Constitution, which had still not reached maturity by the middle of the following year. When on 25 April 1962 the Supreme Soviet set up a commission to draft a new Constitution, the First Secretary of the Party, Khrushchev, indicated some of the matters that the new Constitution should deal with. It should first of all take account of social changes which had taken place since 1936—and in particular it should reflect the nature of present-day Soviet society as an all-nation socialist state engaged on the construction of Communism. It should also reflect the fact that 'proletarian democracy has grown into all-national democracy'; and should take account of the foreign aims of the Soviet Union. Of more interest, perhaps, from the practical point of view, was the First Secretary's suggestion that the new Constitution must raise 'socialist democracy to an even higher level, forming even more solid guarantees of democratic rights and freedoms of the workers and guarantees of the strict observance of socialist legality'. Nothing was said about the projected new Constitution until the end of 1972 when the General Secretary of the CPSU stated that drafting of it was in progress. The draft was, however, not published until 1977: the new Constitution was adapted on 7 October of that year. It made no substantial changes in the structure of Soviet government as described in this book. A short discussion of the 1977 Constitution will be found on pages 170–3.

5

THE FRAMEWORK OF ADMINISTRATION:

ELECTIONS

According to the returns of the census (see the 1971 Year Book of the *Large Soviet Encyclopedia*, pp. 27–29) held in 1970 on 15 January of that year, the population of the Soviet Union totalled 241,700,000. (By July 1975 it had grown to 254,300,000.) At that date the town population exceeded the rural population. The population is young—66·4 per cent of it was under forty on the day of the census and therefore consisted of persons born since the Revolution. The population is very unevenly divided among the fifteen Union republics. Over half the population (133,741,000) now lives in the RSFSR. If the other two republics of Slav population are added, Ukraine (nearly fifty-nine million) and Belorussia (nine million), the three republics together contain over three-quarters of the total population. Only two other republics have substantial populations—Uzbekistan with over thirteen and a half million and Kazakhstan with over fourteen. The remainder range from just under five million—Georgia—to nearly one and a half million—Estonia.

Ninety-one separate nationalities, and as many languages, were listed in the census—the great majority of the national groups being very small. Over a hundred and forty-one million returned Russian as their national language; and if the other Slav language speakers are added—the Ukrainians and the Belorussians—the total exceeds four-fifths of the population. The total percentage of literacy of the population aged between nine and forty-nine, according to the 1970 census returns, was 99·8 per cent (town) and 99·5 per cent (country).

The population figures already show the preponderant position which the RSFSR, and to a much lesser extent the Ukraine, occupy in the country as a whole. Equally impressive (and important for the understanding of the problems of administration in a country which is technically federal in structure) is the concentration of industry in these two republics. Thus, the percentage figures of all workers engaged in industry (in 1970) show that 63·9% were in the RSFSR and 19·1% in the Ukraine—a total of 83% for the whole country. The two republics next in importance in terms of these percentages were Belorussia and Kazakhstan each with 3·3% of all industrial workers. In only five other republics (Uzbekistan, Georgia, Azerbaidjan, Lithuania and Latvia) did the population of industrial workers reach or exceed 1%.

It may not be out of place to list here certain geographical peculiarities of the Soviet Union. Together with the factors contributed by history, they may well have influenced the centralisation which has usually marked the administration of both the Russian Empire and its successor. First, the total territory of the country is vast—one-sixth of the total world land mass. The USSR is three times as large as the United States. Secondly, for its size, the territory is as markedly uniform as western Europe is diversified. According to a leading French geographer of the USSR, its territory 'reduced to its general outlines can be seen in terms of the Russo-Siberian platforms and their mountainous outskirts'. Thirdly, if a few exceptional regions are excluded, the climate is remarkably uniform. Fourthly, this enormous country is essentially land-locked. For its 22,402,200 square kilometres (9 million square miles) of area, it has only 16,000 kilometres (10,000 miles) of sea coast. Moreover, these seas are for the most part either closed, in the sense that they are controlled by other powers—such as the Black Sea or the Baltic—or frozen over for the greater part of the year. It is for this reason that expansion and colonisation by Russia have taken place on land, in the direction of the Ukraine, Poland and the Baltic, and eastwards in Asia.

Finally, nature has endowed the country with exceptionally rich resources, both in quantity and, especially, in diversity. It has been calculated, for example, that of the twenty-six primary materials essential for industry, the USSR has over twenty in sufficient quantities on its own territory—as compared with ten, so far as the USA is concerned. One last fact may be advanced to illustrate the consequences of a highly centralised administration over a period of years. The central region of the USSR, which includes Moscow and Gorky, is the political and administrative heart of the country. Its industrial production exceeds that of any other Soviet industrial area. Yet the area is practically devoid of raw materials and fuel: coal, oil, iron ore and essential metals and minerals have to be brought from other parts of the country. To a great extent, therefore, the industrial growth of the area is a result of deliberate planning.

The broad pattern of the administrative subdivisions of the country becomes apparent when one examines the entire collection of the Constitutions which exist. Apart from that of the USSR, which has been discussed, each of the fifteen Union republics has its own Constitution. But within the Union republics there is a further subdivision, that of the Autonomous Soviet Socialist Republic (ASSR) which is subordinated to the Union republic of the territory of which it forms a part, but enjoys in terms of its constitution a similar autonomy in relation to the Union republic as the latter does in relation to the Union. Autonomous republics are not awarded the 'right' of secession by the Constitution. Nor do autonomous republics enjoy even on paper the right to conduct their own foreign relations or to maintain their own armed forces. Each autonomous republic has its own Constitution which requires approval by the Union republic to which it is subordinated. In contrast, the Constitution of a Union republic is theoretically solely a matter for the republic concerned, and does not require endorsement by the Union. This is provided for by article 19(a) of each Union republican Constitution.

In all there are twenty Constitutions of autonomous republics, in addition to the fifteen Union republican Constitutions—making a total of all Constitutions, together with the All-Union Constitution, of thirty-six. Each group of Constitutions, Union republican and autonomous republican, consists of almost identical documents, with some local variations in addition to the necessary differences of nomenclature. Of the twenty autonomous republics, sixteen are in the RSFSR, namely: the Bashkir ASSR, the Buryat ASSR, the Dagestan ASSR, the Kabardin-Balkar ASSR, the Kalmyk ASSR, the Karelian ASSR, the Komi ASSR, the Mari ASSR, the Mordvin ASSR, the North Osetian ASSR, the Tartar ASSR, the Tuva ASSR, the Udmurt ASSR, the Checheno-Ingush ASSR, the Chuvash ASSR, and the Yakut ASSR; one is in Uzbeki-

stan—the Kara-Kalpak ASSR; two are in Georgia—the Abkhaz-
ian ASSR and the Adjar ASSR; and one in Azerbaidjan—the
Nakhichevan ASSR.

In addition to its sixteen autonomous republics, the vast territory of the RSFSR is composed of six areas (*krai*); five autonomous regions (*avtonomnaya oblast*); and forty-nine administrative
regions (*oblast*). The area is found only in the RSFSR. The main
administrative subdivision of the country is the region. An
autonomous region has no constitution of its own, but sends
deputies to the Council of Nationalities of the Supreme Soviet
(see chapter 6). Those republics which include within their territory autonomous regions (the RSFSR, Georgia, Azerbaidjan and
Tadjikistan) are enjoined by the Constitutions to approve a
directive prepared by the Soviet of the autonomous region or
regions concerned, 'which must take into account the national
peculiarities of the autonomous region' (article 76 of the RSFSR
Constitution—similar articles are to be found in the others,
though in the case of the last-named three republics there is much
greater detail set out in the Constitution on the relations with the
autonomous region).

As of January 1975 there were in all in the USSR 8 autonomous
regions, 6 areas and 120 regions—and these formed the main
administrative divisions of the country. The 120 regions are only
to be found in certain of the republics—49 in the RSFSR, 25 in the
Ukraine, 6 in Belorussia, 11 in Uzbekistan, 19 in Kazakhstan, 5 in
Turkmenistan, 3 in Kirgizia and 2 in Tadjikistan. There also
exists a large administrative subdivision of the area or region,
though mainly it is a historical survival with little practical
importance. This is the national 'circuit' (*okrug*). There are ten of
these, and they are confined to the RSFSR.

The origin of the administrative divisions so far discussed lay in
part in the desire to give effect to national autonomy by providing
gradual degrees of constitutional independence for the ethnic
minorities of the country. This does not, however, apply to the
region (other than the autonomous region) which is historically a
development of the attempts to adapt the administrative divisions
of pre-revolutionary Russia to agricultural needs and to a growing
industrial state. Very broadly, the region is the heir of the old
'government', or *gubernia*, which was placed under a governor in
the Russian Empire. As will be seen below, the modern *oblast* in
the past four years has shown that at any rate as an economic unit

it has proved a failure (see chapter 6). Apart from this factor, the number of regions is a matter which is constantly revised by the central authorities, both for administrative reasons and in some cases perhaps for political reasons—the fewer the regions within a republic, to take one instance, the easier centralised administration becomes. The republics now have full constitutional power to make any administrative changes within their territory and frequently make use of it. For example, since 1953 the number of regions in the RSFSR has been reduced from fifty-five to forty-nine; and in three of the Union republics, Lithuania, Latvia and Estonia, the regions have been abolished. On the other hand, new ones were added in Kazakhstan, Kirgizia, Tadjikistan, Turkmenistan and Uzbekistan.

In order to understand the basic principles of administrative subdivision below the regional tier—i.e. that of the towns and villages—the historical background must be recalled. The emergence of Soviets in all rural areas and towns throughout the country was part of the process of revolution in 1917, and was much exploited by the Bolsheviks in the process of preparing their takeover of power in November. Agricultural collectivisation after 1929 had a double effect: in the first place it rendered, or should have rendered, the rural Soviet largely superfluous, since the functions of rural administration should have largely fallen to the collective farms; moreover, as the collective farms grew in size so the need for a larger rural administrative area than the village became imperative. But the second effect of collectivisation was to increase the gulf between town and village, with the result that town administration was kept separate from that of the surrounding rural areas. Since then much water has flowed under the bridge and the administrative pattern has evolved.

Each republic (and areas and regions where they exist) is divided into districts (*raion*) of which the great majority are rural and a minority urban. (Certain changes were made early in 1963, which are considered together at the end of this chapter.) Thus on 1 January 1975 there were in the whole country 3,097 rural districts and 540 urban or municipal districts. Broadly speaking the rural districts are administrative areas both for the villages and the towns of a particular portion of the country. The urban or municipal districts, on the other hand, are subdivisions of an individual large town, where it is considered necessary to have more than one Soviet. Below the districts come the humbler units—the 'settlements of an urban type', of which there were 3,739 on 1 January 1975, and the rural Soviets, of which there were 41,160.

The towns, of which there were 2,013 in all on 1 January 1962 (nearly half of them in the RSFSR), are subordinated either directly to the republic, the area or the region or circuit (where it exists); or—in the case of the majority of towns, which means the smaller towns—to the appropriate (rural) district. To take the region of Gorky as an example: on 1 January 1974 it had 51 rural districts, each with its 'centre', i.e. either a town or a large village. Within the region there were 25 towns, of which 11, including Gorky itself (the centre of regional administration) were directly subordinate to the region. The remaining 14, each of which was also a 'district centre', were subordinate to one of the rural districts. There were also 8 urban or municipal districts—i.e. subdivisions of the larger towns of over 100,000 population; and 65 settlements of urban type.

Each of these units, from the village upwards, is characterised by the fact that it is entitled to elect a Soviet. The functions of these Soviets, the extent to which they enjoy any degree of autonomy and the nature of subordination, are all discussed in chapter 7. So far as constitutional law is concerned, it must largely be derived from the network of constitutions where the powers at each level are set out. Another problem with which the Soviet authorities have been much preoccupied in past years is the relationship of the existing administrative system to the problem of both industrial and agricultural planning, control and management. To these matters it will also be necessary to turn at a later stage (see chapter 6). But even before these questions are dealt with, reference must be made to certain trends in the matter of local administration which became apparent by the end of 1962 and which made it possible to predict the broad line along which local administration was likely to develop in the near future.

In the first place it looked as if the rural district had outlived its usefulness, and was for the most part scheduled for abolition. It will be recalled that in November 1962 the party resolved on a new system of local party organs which, from the level of the region downwards, would give more effect to the production principle, with the result that (in most cases) within one region there were to be party organs of varying jurisdiction dealing respectively with industrial and with agricultural control and guidance. In the process the existing party rural district committees were destined to disappear, and to give way to larger organs varying in size according as they are concerned with industry or with agriculture within a particular region (see chapter 3). At the same time a number of authoritative statements were made suggesting that a similar subdivision into two would be made for the Soviets at the regional level; and that the rural district would no longer survive as an administrative area at all.

The administrative changes which were made after November 1962 fell broadly under two heads, and closely paralleled the changes made in the party network. In the first place, wherever the regional party committees had been split into separate industrial and agricultural party committees, there took place a corresponding bifurcation of the Soviet into an industrial and an agricultural Soviet. In the RSFSR the Soviets of five out of the six areas and thirty-seven out of the forty-nine regions were divided up in this manner, in the Ukraine nineteen out of twenty-five, in Uzbekistan four out of eight, the one in Kirgizia, all six in Belorussia and three out of fifteen in Kazakhstan. The principle governing the decision to leave regional Soviets undivided (such as the six western regions of the Ukraine) seems to have been to leave unchanged regions which are almost entirely agricultural.

The existence of two Soviets in the majority of the regions was bound to engender administrative confusion and overlapping. It was therefore not to be wondered at that when, after the fall of Khrushchev, the whole of his reform of the party organisation (for which there was at all events some justification on the grounds of rationality) was swept away, the cumbersome system of divided soviets should have come to an end as well.

The position with the district (*raion*) was however rather different. Quite apart from party politics or the personal idiosyncrasies of rulers, the district, as it existed in 1962, had outlived its usefulness as an administrative organ at the rural level. Little change, other than the routine readjustments of boundaries which go on all the time, has taken place since 1962 so far as the cities or, rather, so far as the urban districts, which are administrative subdivisions of the cities, are concerned. But the number of rural districts, of which there were 3,421 in 1962, has been considerably reduced. Already by 1963 the total number was only 1,287. The geographical extent of each of the new enlarged rural districts was designed to correspond to the areas of the new authorities set up in March 1962 for the administration of agriculture—the 'kolkhoz-

sovkhoz production directorates' (or 'sovkhoz-kolkhoz production directorates' where state farms predominated). As conceived
of by Khrushchev, these directorates were to be joint party-state
bodies. As part of their organisation, they were designed to
incorporate a party committee which would function as an integral
part of the whole directorate, and which would replace the *raion*
party committee, which was abolished. This measure, which was
very unpopular in the party apparatus, did not survive the fall of
Khrushchev, and the *raion* party committees were restored in
November 1964. However, something of Khrushchev's administrative reform of the districts has survived, since the number of
rural administrative districts in January 1975 was still considerably smaller (2,557) than it was in 1962.

At the basis of all the Soviets to which reference has been made,
and at the basis of the Supreme Soviet of the USSR (which will be
discussed in the next chapter), lies the electoral system. This is
covered by ch. XI of the Constitution and by the Electoral Laws
enacted in conformity with it. The Constitution only lays down
certain basic principles, which are stated to apply to elections to
all Soviets—from the Supreme Soviets of the USSR, the Union
republics and the autonomous republics, through the Soviets of
areas, regions, autonomous regions, circuits, districts and towns,
right down to the villages. Voting is secret and direct and the
suffrage is universal and equal. These principles were enacted for
the first time in the Constitution of 1936 (article 134). The earlier
Constitutions—apart from a preference for open voting which
was then said to be more 'democratic'—were based on unequal
suffrage and indirect voting. Thus certain categories of persons,
considered hostile to the new Soviet regime, such as priests or
those exploiting the labour of others, were denied the franchise
already in the first Constitution of the RSFSR of 1918. Representation was indirect in the sense that the supreme legislature, the
All-Union Congress of Soviets, was by the terms of the first
Union (USSR) Constitution of 1924 elected indirectly by the
delegates of the Soviets lower down the scale. Representation was
also unequal up to 1936 in the sense that the town electors were
given a preference in the voting over the village electors. (Thus,
by article 9 of ch. III of the Constitution of 1924, one deputy was
elected for every 25,000 electors in the towns and one deputy for
every 125,000 inhabitants in the villages. In other words, the town

vote was given perhaps three times the effect of the village vote.) The abolition of these voting restrictions, together with the introduction of secret voting, were much vaunted in 1936 as signs of the democratic nature of the Soviet regime, the popularity of the party and its leaders, and the political maturity of the electors. The unprecedented scale, even for Soviet conditions, on which purges were conducted against the entire population between 1936 and 1938, forces one to look for another explanation for the changes. This would seem to be that the Soviet leaders (or more accurately Stalin) could afford to give to a new Constitution these outward democratic forms because they (or he) were fully confident of the ability of their administrative organisation—the party—effectively to control the elections.

All Soviet citizens who have reached the age of eighteen are entitled to vote without distinction of race, sex, ethnic or social origin, past or present activity or the extent of their property. Any citizen of twenty-three and over, once again without any of the distinctions enumerated, can be elected a Supreme Soviet deputy. Since 1958 only the insane are denied the vote (article 135). Candidates are nominated by constituencies: the right to nominate candidates for election to the Soviets is reserved to 'public organisations and the toilers' societies', namely, 'the Communist Party organisations, the trade unions, co-operatives, youth organisations and cultural societies' (article 141). Individuals have no right to nominate. Finally, every deputy is obliged to give an account of his activity to his electors, and can be recalled at any time by a decision of a majority of those electors (article 142).

For those who are inclined to accept paper guarantees which are not enshrined in strong and independently functioning institutions, ch. XI of the 1936 Constitution, so far as drafting is concerned, seems a much more convincing document than ch. X on Rights and Duties. When the regulations for the first Supreme Soviet elections were published in 1937 it was observed that provision was made (as it still is) for contested elections: the voter was instructed to cross out all names on the ballot paper except the name of the one candidate for whom he desired to vote. Stalin himself added to the fun by telling a foreign newspaper correspondent that he anticipated lively, contested elections with several candidates competing.

When the list of candidates appeared there was in fact only one candidate offering himself in each constituency—either a Communist or a non-party member of the 'bloc of Communist and non-party' candidates. Although the instructions on the ballot paper have remained the same since then, in the thirty-one years that have elapsed since 1937, in no single instance has more than one candidate been put forward in any constituency in any Supreme Soviet election—nor, so far as is known, in the election to any other lower Soviet.

The organisation of Supreme Soviet elections, at any rate, has left nothing to be desired. Throughout this period the overwhelming majority of the electors went to the polls, to an extent which is completely unknown in any parliamentary or presidential system of government where election can be demonstrated to be reasonably free. Thus in 1937 96·8% of all electors went to the polls in the first Supreme Soviet election, in 1946 99·7% and in 1958 and 1966 the percentages were respectively 99·97 and 99·94. On each and every occasion similar majorities were cast for the single list of candidates of the party and non-party bloc. The Soviet leaders frequently cite figures such as those quoted above as evidence of the greater degree to which democracy obtains in the Soviet Union than in, say, Britain or the USA; and as evidence of the full support and confidence which the party enjoys in the eyes of the Soviet population. That they do not even themselves take such an assertion very seriously is proved by one grotesque little incident. In 1938 the Volga Germans voted in elections to the republican Supreme Soviet: 99·8% of them went to the polls, 99·7% voted for the official bloc candidate. Three years later the entire community of Volga Germans was accused of harbouring 'tens of thousands of deviationists and spies' and deported *en masse*. Similar figures could be cited for the other nationalities deported for alleged disloyalty during the war and since 'rehabilitated'.

When the two stages of a Soviet election—nomination and voting—are examined in detail, the degree of control by the party becomes apparent. Indeed Soviet writers on government would not deny this, nor is control by the party regarded by Soviet writers on constitutional law as anything improper—it is indeed fully consistent with Lenin's doctrine, and in particular his fear of the 'spontaneity' of the masses, unless led by their vanguard, the party.

For the purpose of nominating and electing candidates in the

elections to the Supreme Soviet, the country is divided into
constituencies. These are different for elections to the two chambers of the Supreme Soviet. According to the Constitution (article
34) the Council of the Union is to be composed of one deputy for
every three hundred thousand inhabitants, and the constituencies
are created accordingly. But the Council of Nationalities is composed in another manner—thirty-two deputies from each Union
republic, eleven from each autonomous republic, five from each
autonomous region, and one from each national circuit or *okrug*
(article 35). The division into constituencies is in accordance with
these provisions. Thus a voter will always have to vote twice in a
Supreme Soviet election—once for each chamber; but if he
happens to live in an autonomous unit within a republic he will
vote thrice, that is to say, once for the Council of the Union
deputy and once each for the separate autonomous unit and
republican representatives in the Council of Nationalities. (The
ballot forms are in practice of different colours.) For purposes of
voting and counting of votes the constituencies are divided into
polling districts, which are the same for both chambers. These
polling districts are normally organised at the rate of one district
for 2,000–3,000 inhabitants, except in the very sparsely populated
far north and east. Local polling districts are set up in army units,
in hospitals and in trains.

For control over both the nominations of candidates and of
polling a system of electoral commissions is maintained. These
commissions are set up for the purpose of seeing that nominations
and elections are conducted in accordance with the laws, and they
are the sole and final judges in all cases of complaint—both in the
matter of nominations and of polling. There is no appeal to or
supervision by the courts. The electoral commissions consist of a
central commission and of local commissions in every constituency and in every polling district. These commissions are not,
according to the law, elected: they are 'composed' or 'formed'
(both words are used in the statute) of representatives of broadly
the same organisations as the ones entitled to nominate candidates for election. The statute is silent on the question of who
'composes' or 'forms' the electoral commission and how it is done.
In practice they normally consist of party members and of persons
who can be trusted to carry out the wishes of the party. The all-
important secretary of an electoral commission is invariably an
important party member.

Although the right to nominate candidates is allowed by the Constitution to a number of organisations, the role of the party is of paramount importance—indeed it could scarcely be otherwise, because the party (as another article of the Constitution points out —article 126) is the 'leading core' of every one of these organisations. The role of the party is primarily to ensure that its own candidate is nominated. A recent (1957) directive of the Central Committee enjoins party organisations when putting forward candidates for election to the Soviets to agree them first with 'the workers and peasants' and then to put forward a single candidate. This procedure may well occur: it is extremely unlikely in Soviet conditions that the party will have much difficulty in ensuring the acceptance of its own candidate, except occasionally at the lowest levels. Cases occur (sometimes several hundred) in local Soviet elections where the official candidate does not receive the required majority (50% plus one vote) and a second election (presumably with another candidate) has to take place. But in the case of the Supreme Soviet such an occurrence is inconceivable in present conditions. The party is sufficiently well able to control the organisations concerned to ensure that the required candidate is nominated and elected. Indeed, as will be seen later, the composition of the Supreme Soviet reflects a definite pattern, based on office and on public and social status, which is sufficiently uniform over the years to make it certain beyond doubt that some element at least of central planning of candidatures is involved (see chapter 6). There is ample evidence in the files of the Smolensk party organisation, which fell into Allied hands during the war, of directives by the party on who should be 'elected'. It is possible that in some cases within the framework of a general central directive some allowance is made for the wishes of the local population. After selection the candidate must be registered by the electoral commission. Since this is the final instance which has the power of deciding on the validity of nominations a further stage of official control is thus provided.

Polling always takes place on a Sunday from 6 a.m. until 10 p.m. A considerable propaganda effort is devoted to getting people to the polls. Literally millions of party members and active party supporters are engaged both to conduct propaganda in the weeks before the elections and to encourage voters to go to the polls on election day—the success of their efforts has already been noted. It will be observed that in an electoral district of a maximum size of 3,000 it is not very difficult for the local party officials to know who has absented himself from the polling station. The polling station is in charge of and under the control of the district electoral commission, and one (or more) of its members is present all day. In each polling station private voting cabins or rooms must be provided 'for the filling up of their voting bulletins by the voters', to quote the election law. No one other than the voter is allowed in the voting room or cabin—exception only being made for the illiterate or physically handicapped who require assistance. These provisions are the essentials of any fair system of voting. But it is here that the importance of the single candidate becomes apparent. The voter is officially instructed to cross out the names of all candidates except the name of the one for whom he wishes to vote, and then to drop his ballot paper into the ballot box. But with one single name invariably on the ballot paper there is in fact nothing for the voter to cross out. All that the voter who is prepared to vote for the official candidate has to do is to drop his paper into the ballot box unmarked in any way whatever. It follows from this that anyone who in fact retires to the private cabin immediately draws attention to himself, since he can only wish to do so in order to cross out the single name on the paper or to write something on the ballot paper which will in some other way indicate dissent. Such an open indication of dissent, in a small district voting office, in the presence of the local party officials, or at least of the electoral commission officers, is an act of defiance which, naturally enough, few Soviet voters are anxious to commit. The figures cited above are eloquent proof of the efficacy of the system. It is, incidentally, probable that such figures are genuine, since representatives of the press and public organisations are entitled to be present at the count. However much these representatives may be selected for their trustworthiness, it is less likely now than in the past that blatant electoral fraud could be practised in the presence of so many witnesses. A heavy penalty is in fact provided by the electoral law for cases of electoral fraud in preparing returns by members of the electoral commission.

The Soviet election must thus be viewed as serving some purpose other than the 'selection' of representatives which in a free parliamentary or presidential system of government is regarded as its actual main function. In Britain or in the USA, for example, the nature of the future government of the country depends upon the result of the General or Presidential election. In the USSR this position seems rather to be reversed—the nature of the government, the controlling, self-perpetuating party leadership determines the result of the elections. Soviet writers claim that the virtually unanimous support of a single candidate election after election proves that the Soviet electorate, unlike that of Britain or the USA, is not divided by dissensions and by class divisions. But so long as Soviet elections are controlled by the party, which has a vested interest in perpetuating its own rule, the truth or falsehood of this claim cannot be put to the test.

What then is the purpose of a Soviet general election, if not to form a government? There would seem to be three main purposes. First, it is a public demonstration of the legitimacy of the regime— the great plebiscites which dictators have so frequently organised in the past served exactly the same purpose. Secondly, an election in Soviet conditions is an invaluable educational and propaganda exercise. It provides experience in mass indoctrination for millions of party and non-party activists. It provides a good opportunity to stress the wisdom and achievements of the party in the past and to disseminate its promises for the even more glorious future. Thirdly, and perhaps most important of all, it provides proof that the system of control is unimpaired—the voters have been once again brought to the polls, and the overwhelming majority of them have voted the right way. The dread 'spontaneity' has been averted once again. So by this ritual, for it is at present little more than a ritual, the Soviet Union renews its spiritual forces in the tradition of the great Lenin every time that a new Supreme Soviet is elected.

6

CENTRAL GOVERNMENT

The organs of central All-Union Government are described in chs. III and V of the Constitution. Soviet constitutional thought does not recognise the separation of powers as a cardinal principle. When the Soviets first came into being as revolutionary organs the fact that they symbolised 'the people' in its uncomplicated political activity, in which there was no need to draw any distinction between the executive and the legislative side of their work, was much vaunted as proof of their superiority over the bourgeois forms of government. Things have changed, and government in the USSR is at the least no less complex than anywhere else. Necessity alone dictates the need for some form of specialisation in government activity. So the constitution recognises separate legislative and executive organs, with distinct spheres of action. However the theory which pays scant respect to separation of powers as a principle is perhaps still reflected both in the general structure of Soviet central government and often in the absence, in practice, of a clear demarcation line between the two spheres of government activity. This is in truth no more than a reflection of the reality, for behind the formal organs of government now being considered stands the real source of both legislative and executive power—the party.

The 'supreme organ of state power' in the USSR according to article 30 of the Constitution is the Supreme Soviet of the USSR. In it are vested the 'exclusive' power of legislation (article 32); and the exercise of all state powers vested in the government of the USSR under article 14 (see chapter 4) in so far as these are not, by the terms of the Constitution, vested either in the Praesidium of the Supreme Soviet or in the Council of Ministers or Ministries of the USSR (article 31). The Supreme Soviet is bicameral in structure, consisting of the Council of the Union in which each delegate represents 300,000 inhabitants of the Union; and of the Council of Nationalities, in which the Union and autonomous republics as well as the autonomous regions (and the surviving National Circuits) are each represented by, respectively, 32, 11, 5 and 1 deputies (articles 33 to 35). The two chambers are equal in rights, and in particular enjoy equal rights of legislative initiative. The sessions of each chamber begin and end at the same time (articles 37, 38 and 41). There is also provision for joint sessions (article 45).

Each Supreme Soviet is elected for four years and is required to meet twice a year. But extraordinary sessions may be summoned by the Praesidium or at the request of any one Union republic (articles 36 and 46). In order to be valid a law, or statute, of the Supreme Soviet requires a simple majority of votes in each chamber. In the event of a disagreement between the two chambers the matter must be transferred to a conciliation commission on which both chambers are equally represented. If the conciliation commission fails to achieve agreement between the two chambers, the question is once more debated in both chambers. If the result is still a failure of the two chambers to agree, the Praesidium must dissolve the Supreme Soviet and fix a date for a new election (articles 39 and 47). These elaborate provisions have so far remained quite academic. Since the first Supreme Soviet met under the terms of the present Constitution in 1937 there has been no recorded instance in which any decision of the Supreme Soviet has been reached otherwise than by a completely unanimous vote of both chambers.

Since the Supreme Soviet seldom meets more than twice a year and has in the past met even less frequently than that; and since its sessions usually last only a few days, it follows that even the formal work of legislation must fall upon other organs. One of these is the Praesidium of the Supreme Soviet, which is elected by both chambers in joint session. It consists of a Chairman, fifteen deputy chairmen—one from each Union republic; a secretary; and twenty members (article 48). Although the constitutional powers of the Praesidium are vested in the whole body, in practice every state requires a titular head, if only for ceremonial purposes

—such as the accrediting of ambassadors or the formal reception of the visits of heads of foreign states. In the USSR these titular functions are usually performed by the chairman of the Praesidium of the Supreme Soviet. The fifteen deputy presidents are usually the fifteen presidents of the Praesidia of the Supreme Soviets of the Union republics. (At a time when the total number of Union republics was sixteen, that is to say before the Karelian-Finnish Soviet Socialist Republic became the Karelian Autonomous Soviet Socialist Republic and was reduced in status in 1956, the total number of deputy chairmen was also sixteen.) The twenty members of the Praesidium usually include some important high party dignitaries who do not otherwise enjoy high state office, and are thus given a government as distinct from a party status. The secretary is provided with an office, which ensures the continuous existence and functioning of the Praesidium at the time, which is most of the time, when the Supreme Soviet itself is not in session. In practice this body in permanent session includes, in addition to the secretary and his staff, a small number of the more important Praesidium members, sometimes collectively known as the 'Small Praesidium'. (It may be observed that the members of the Praesidium include important party leaders, among them the First Secretary of the Central Committee.)

The eighteen functions of the Praesidium, enumerated in article 49, may be divided broadly into legislative and executive functions. Among the legislative functions the most important is that of issuing decrees. The Constitution does not lay down any rules which require that the decrees of the Praesidium must be ratified by the Supreme Soviet. However, in so far as a decree operates, as very many of them do, to create entirely new law, or even in some cases to enact new law which is in conflict with the provisions of the Constitution, the need for ratification may be said to be implied. Indeed, article 32 confers on the Supreme Soviet (and not on its Praesidium) the exclusive right of legislation. But in practice the great bulk of legislation in the Soviet Union issues in the first instance from the Praesidium in the form of a decree. The majority of these decrees are ratified by the Supreme Soviet in full session, though this is usually a purely formal act. Where necessary a constitutional amendment will be adopted, for which a two-thirds majority is required under article 146. It should however be noted that the decree of the Praesidium comes into force immediately, and remains in force even though (as has sometimes happened) ratification or constitutional amendment is delayed for years.

Among the functions of the Praesidium related to that of legislation are three which are seldom known to have been exercised in practice. These are: the authoritative interpretation of the laws of the USSR; the conduct of a national referendum, either on its own initiative or on that of one Union republic; and setting aside the Rules and Orders made by the Council of Ministers either of the USSR or of the Union republics in the event of their being 'in conflict with the law'. But one function is most frequently exercised—the appointment or removal of Ministers of the USSR. This is done on the initiative of the Chairman of the Council of Ministers of the USSR, and each change requires (and in practice always receives) ratification by the Supreme Soviet.

The purely executive functions of the Praesidium comprise the following: the creation and conferment of titles, honours and other marks of rank and distinction, military, diplomatic and civilian; the exercise of the right of mercy; the appointment and removal of the supreme command of the armed forces; declaration of war in between sessions of the Supreme Soviet 'in the event of an armed attack on the USSR' or in the event of the necessity of fulfilling an obligation under a treaty of mutual defence against aggression; mobilisation; ratification and denunciation of treaties; the appointment of envoys to foreign states and the reception of envoys accredited to the USSR; and the declaration of martial law in case of need in the interest either of national defence or national security.

The Supreme Soviet has become a body of substantial size, as the following details of the results of the elections held in March 1962 will show. Of the total of over 140 million of those entitled to vote, 99·95% voted. The official list of candidates from the 'people's bloc of party and non-party members' comprised a total of 1,443 names, and all were elected: 791 as deputies to the Soviet of the Union and 652 as deputies to the Soviet of Nationalities. The percentages of those who voted in favour of the list were: in the 791 polling constituencies for the Council of the Union 99·47%; in the 652 polling constituencies for the Soviet of Nationalities 99·6%. Analysis of the occupations of the deputies showed a less official and more popularly based composition of this Supreme Soviet as compared with previous elections. Thus, manual workers formed 45% of the deputies, as compared with

33% in 1958 and only 19% in 1954. It was also significant that nearly two-thirds of the deputies in this Soviet were elected for the first time, and that the number of younger deputies had also increased since 1958. The broader popular base of this Soviet did not however mean that the senior party and government officials were under-represented. All members and candidate members of the Praesidium of the party were elected, all the Central Committee secretaries and seventeen senior officials of the central party apparatus. The 226 republican and provincial party secretaries made up 16% of the deputies. Of the seventy-five members of the Council of Ministers (in March 1962) all but fourteen were elected deputies. Military and police representation formed 4·5% and deputies from the intelligentsia 10%. All in all, it was plain that those who plan the lists of approved candidates labour to ensure fair representation of important sections of official life; but it was also plain that this time more care was taken to represent wider and less official sections as well.

It would be difficult to imagine a body of this size and composition engaging in serious legislative activity, and indeed it does not, except in the most formal sense. The second session of this Soviet was held in 1962 between 10 and 13 December, both days inclusive—a total of four working days. Two days were devoted to long reports and debate on the Plan and budget for 1963. No single criticism of either was made in debate and both were adopted unanimously. The last two days were mainly devoted to a long report on foreign policy by the First Secretary of the party and the chairman of the Council of Ministers (Mr Khrushchev) to a joint session of both houses, followed by 'debate' of similar nature and the unanimous adoption by both houses of an approving resolution. On the last day, however, a series of decrees of the Praesidium were ratified. These comprised: ten decrees relating to the reorganisation of the government machinery, necessitating consequential amendments to three articles of the Constitution; fourteen decrees relating to ministerial appointments issued by the Praesidium in the past six months; and four decrees concerning military service, rates of pay in the Far East, income tax and administrative fines. None of these was debated. These figures are typical of elections held in subsequent years and of the work of the Supreme Soviet.

It must be plain by now that wherever Soviet legislation may take place it cannot be at the public sessions of the Supreme Soviet, which is at most a declaratory and ratifying body. It follows that the stage of legislation which matters in the Soviet Union is the preparatory stage. The practice of the past few years suggests that this preparatory stage takes place in a variety of ways. It is obvious that major legislative measures must necessarily originate in the party, since it is the party which is responsible for policy leadership. The party possesses a relatively small but highly qualified technical apparatus in its Secretariat with its departments. For further technical co-operation the party can look to the Council of Ministers or to the individual departments specialising in the field concerned. Indeed many of the major legislative proposals in the past few years have been publicly launched in the form of joint resolutions of the Council of Ministers of the USSR and of the Central Committee of the CPSU, even though in some (not all) cases they may have been followed by the required formal enactment in statutory form by the Supreme Soviet.

The Supreme Soviet is therefore at most a confirming body and can play little if any part as a sounding board for opinion in the country. Less formal methods are available for seeking such public co-operation when the party and government leaders think it desirable. Discussion in the press of draft proposals has become more usual in recent years than it was in the past. There is no doubt much informal and unpublicised consultation with the public in, at any rate, some cases, including consultation with the relevant authorities in the Union republics. Finally, a number of legislative measures are discussed in draft form in the permanent commissions which are set up by each chamber of the Supreme Soviet. Leaving aside the mandates commission of each chamber which is charged with the duty of ensuring that deputies have been duly elected and which furnishes statistical and other information on the deputies, there are the following parallel commissions in all: planning and budget; industry, transport and communications; construction and building materials industry; agriculture; health and national insurance; education, culture and sport; trade and services; legislation, foreign affairs; youth affairs.

Before 1966 there were six parallel commissions: foreign affairs, budget, and legislation. In addition, from 1957 onwards the Soviet of Nationalities had an economic commission, which reflected the increased amount of responsibility entrusted to the Union republics.

The commissions are appointed for the whole life of the Supreme Soviet. They may meet more frequently than the open sessions, and sit for longer periods. Their activity is not public,

and they have fairly wide powers of access to documents, to
ministries and to ministers, and of enlisting the assistance of outside persons whose experience may be of help to them. Their
powers are purely consultative and amount in practice to little
more than persuasion: in the last resort, like every other institution in the Soviet Union, the party can easily enforce discipline
and obedience on them should they be tempted to step too far in
the direction of independent action. But it may fairly be assumed
that in some instances at any rate they are in a position to influence the general shape of legislation in the matter of practical
detail. In particular, the budget and economic commissions of the
Council of Nationalities can perhaps play some small part in
safeguarding the interests of the Union republics (see chapter 7).
The commissions enjoy the advantage that their activities do not
take place in public, where Soviet tradition and practice demand
complete unanimity, interpreting even minor dissent as insupport-
able criticism of the leaders' policy. It is therefore more easy for
them, within the limits of tact and caution, at times to engage in
real discussion. However, the results of their deliberations when
presented to the Supreme Soviet are always unanimous and, in
the cases where a project has been discussed in the parallel commissions of each chamber, identical.

The only qualification laid down for a deputy to the Supreme
Soviet is that he should be over twenty-three years of age. When
elected he enjoys the right to draw his salary from his place of
employment while engaged on his duties, expenses for transport
and other emoluments. He is immune from criminal prosecution
or arrest without the authority of the Supreme Soviet, or of the
Praesidium when the Supreme Soviet is not in session (article
52). The Constitution imposes upon him the duty of accounting
to his constituents, and provides for his recall from office should
they be dissatisfied with his conduct (article 142). This provision is
of little practical importance to the electors, who can have as little
say in the process of recall as in the process of nomination of a
candidate—both being entirely subordinate to party control.
Moreover, in many instances deputies are busy party or government officials with little time to devote to their constituents.
However, within these limits, there is no doubt that many deputies
take their duties as intermediaries between the public and the state
machine seriously, listen to complaints and grievances, intercede
informally in individual cases and do their best to advance the

legitimate local interests of their constituency. As in some parliaments in other countries, the private and unseen function of the deputy may well be of more use to the public than his formal and visible functions.

The Council of Ministers of the USSR is described in article 64 (of ch. V) of the Constitution as the 'supreme executive and directing organ of state power'. It is the successor to the original Council of People's Commissars, the change of name having been made in 1946. It is responsible to the Supreme Soviet, and between its sessions, to the Praesidium (article 65). It is not in theory endowed with powers of legislation, but may only issue 'ordinances and directives on the basis of and in fulfilment of existing valid legislation' (article 66). In practice these ordinances are often indistinguishable from new legislation, and undoubtedly effect changes in the law. In the absence of any process of judicial review in the USSR these ordinances are in practice never challenged, and enjoy, by the terms of article 67, validity in the entire territory of the USSR. (They may, in theory, however, be set aside by the Praesidium, under article 49.) It should also be noted that the All-Union Council of Ministers enjoys a pre-eminence over Union republican Councils of Ministers and over the Councils of National Economy, since, within the spheres of activity assigned to the competence of the Union, it can set aside the ordinances of these local bodies (article 69).

The All-Union Council of Ministers is a very large body.* Its composition varies a great deal from time to time, reflecting the changes in administrative policy, and in the power relationship between the Union and the Union republics. It is generally composed of its chairman; of first deputy and of deputy chairmen; of All-Union and Union republican ministers; of the chairmen of State Committees, with or without ministerial status; of the chairmen of other important state bodies, like the Supreme Council of National Economy or the State Bank; and of the chairmen of the Councils of Ministers of the fifteen Union republics *ex officio*.

Before considering the functions of the Council of Ministers as a whole it may be useful to look at the holders of some of the various offices who compose it. The chairman of the Council of Ministers (or Prime Minister as he may be called) is usually the

* See Appendix for its composition.

linch pin of the whole party-state system, because it now appears more usual than not for the office to be combined with the highest party office—that of First Secretary. Stalin combined the two offices for much of his career; and Khrushchev, who became First Secretary some months after Stalin's death in March 1953, added to his party office the government office of Prime Minister in March 1958. He had, in the previous June, successfully out-witted his rivals for power in the party Praesidium and their defeat was crowned by a vote of the Central Committee of the Party; and the assumption of the additional office of Prime Minister, hitherto held by Bulganin who had opposed Khrushchev in the Praesidium, was thus the final consolidation of this victory. The first deputy chairmen and the deputy chairmen are usually ministers without portfolio, exercising a high degree of reponsi-bility in the co-ordination of branches of national administration. The Prime Minister and his deputies together form the Praesidium of the Council of Ministers of the USSR—a kind of 'Inner Cabinet' in which the real policy making of the Council takes place. In view of the unwieldy character of the Council of Ministers the existence of such an inner body is plainly a necessity—indeed it is not certain that the full Council of Ministers ever meets. It is not known if the Praesidium of the Council of Ministers ever includes other ministers or chairmen of State Committees, but it seems probable.

Ministries at the Union level are of two kinds—All-Union and Union-republican. All-Union ministries are in sole charge within their field of competence of the sphere of administration entrusted to them, without reference to the republican governments. These ministries can act directly throughout the USSR, if necessary through local organs or branches appointed by and directly res-ponsible to themselves. Union-republican ministries as a general rule are central ministries which have corresponding Union-republican ministries in the republics. (As will be seen below, there are also republican ministries which have no counterpart in Moscow.)

Between 1957 and 1965 there was a trend towards the reduction of the number of All-Union ministries. Some of them became Union-republican. In other cases Union-republican ministries were abolished and the sphere of administration left within the competence of the republics—Justice, for example, or Mainten-ance of Public Order (not to be confused with State Security, which has always been, and still is, completely centralised.) This trend must be seen in conjunction with the reorganisation in 1957 of the control over industry through a system of regional Councils of National Economy, which is described below. At the same time there took place a proliferation of State Committees of the Council of Ministers at the All-Union level. Most of these State Committees, unlike the Ministries which they replaced, were not intended to administer enterprises, but to co-ordinate production, to plan distribution and utilisation of resources, and in particular to co-ordinate, encourage and supervise the development of technological study within the particular branch entrusted to them. This system was abandoned in 1965, and the more traditional pattern of administering the nationalised economy through a number of All-Union and Union-Republican ministries was reverted to. Centralisation was also restored in other areas; for example, the Union Republican Ministry for the Maintenance of Public Order has been restored and renamed Ministry of the Interior (November 1968).

The importance of the All-Union Council of Ministers is twofold. In the first place it is the apex of administrative and executive control over the resources of a country in which all industry is nationalised and agriculture, though much of it technically 'co-operative', is in practice more or less constantly controlled by the state. Secondly, it is the centre from which the economy is planned. The Council of Ministers is for this purpose closely integrated with the top party leadership by the fact that its leading members are usually also the leading members of the supreme party instance—the Politburo of the Central Committee—and for substantial periods in Soviet history its chairman has been the First (or General) Secretary of the party, who is also the Chairman of the Party Politburo. In view of its size it is improbable that it ever meets as a whole, or that such plenary meetings, if they do take place, are anything more than a formality. It exercises its effect on policy either through its Praesidium or through improvised and informal sub-committees of its more important members, usually in close conjunction with the central apparatus of the party.

One of the most important functions of the All-Union Council of Ministers is to co-ordinate the national industrial plan, and to ensure its execution by industrial enterprises throughout the country. This function is closely related to the system of organisation of industry. In 1957 it was decided to make severe inroads on what had hitherto been the traditional system for the control of industry—almost complete centralisation of control at the All-Union level, with each branch of industry controlled separately. This system, apart from the excessive centralisation involved which left little initiative to the Union republics (though in this respect the republics had been gradually acquiring more control over industry from 1954 onwards) also suffered from several other disadvantages. The most important of these were three.

First, the system which had prevailed hitherto of controlling each branch of industry in a self-contained ministry was becoming unworkable in the face of the growing complexity of the economy. The State Planning Committee, *Gosplan*, was not strong enough to ensure effective co-ordination, with resultant waste of effort and resources. Secondly, no effective authority was responsible for regional planning, in spite of some strengthening of the power of the republics—for one thing, it will be recalled that the very in-equality in size and industrial potential of the republics makes them totally unsuitable as economic regions. And thirdly, concentration of too much authority in Moscow was the source of intolerable bureaucratic delay and confusion.

However, the economic reorganisation which was enacted in May 1957 was only in part due to these practical reasons. At least one of the motives behind it was the aim of the First Secretary of the Communist Party, N. S. Khrushchev, to assert his own authority and that of the senior party apparatus against the less ideologically minded planners. This became evident a few months later after the political downfall of the serious opposition to Khrushchev which had formed within the party Praesidium (headed by Malenkov, Kaganovich and Molotov, but supported by several leading planners like Saburov and Pervukhin). As will be seen below, this political factor determined certain features of the reorganisation of 1957.

The general character of the reform in May 1957 was an attempt to combine the advantages of overall central planning with a measure of regional autonomy. No less than ten All-Union and thirteen Union republican ministries in Moscow were abolished. The country was divided into 105 economic regions—seventy in the RSFSR, eleven in the Ukraine, four in Uzbekistan, nine in Kazakhstan, and one each in the remaining republics. A Council of National Economy (*Sovnarkhoz*) was placed at the head of each region and made responsible for all industrial undertakings within the region, with two exceptions: first, about 6% of industry, mainly of a defence character, remained subordinated directly to All-Union ministries; and secondly, local industry remained, as hitherto, under the control of the administrative regions (*oblasti*). The Councils of National Economy were subordinated to the republican Councils of Ministers. The general co-ordination of industry within the republics was entrusted to the republican State Planning Committees, and overall planning to the All-Union State Planning Committee (*Gosplan*).

Several features of this system were evidently dictated by political rather than economic considerations, and the system as a whole already contained within it the seeds of future tribulations. In the first place the selection of the original 105 economic regions was dictated, in part at any rate, by a desire not to interfere too much with the domain and authority of the powerful first secretaries of the regional (*oblast*) party committees. Hence the economic regions tended to a large extent (though not entirely) to coincide with the existing administrative regions, where economic considerations often demanded quite different regionalisation. Secondly, the subordination of the Councils of National Economy solely to the republican Councils of Ministers (and not, as originally intended, both to the republican and to the All-Union Councils of Ministers) gave the republics greater authority than was reconcilable with the desire to maintain a centrally determined national plan for industry. This in turn threw even more responsibility on the party organs at the regional level, since their officials (and in particular their first secretaries) could be expected to ensure that central policy was given priority over local or republican interests.

Things did not work out that way. Before long what was to become the main complaint against the new system—'localism', or putting the local before the national interest—was extended to some of the regional party first secretaries as well as to the Councils of National Economy. In the year which followed the reform of 1957 there were clear trends visible towards more central control and towards greater rationalisation of the economic regions. Many of the abolished All-Union ministries returned in the guise of State Committees attached to the All-Union Council of Ministers or of powerfully expanded industrial departments of the All-Union *Gosplan*. The number of economic regions was reduced and co-ordinating bodies were set up. Moreover there were evident signs that many of the first secretaries of regional party committees were falling into disfavour.

At the end of 1962 and at the beginning of 1963 the system was completely reorganised. (The ministerial reorganisation must be seen in conjunction with the reorganisation of the party machinery on production branch lines, which was described in chapter 3.) In general, the aim of the reorganisation seems to have been two-fold: to eliminate by increased centralisation of planning and control the trends towards 'localism' which had become increasingly apparent since 1957; and to reduce the effects of excessive lack of co-ordination between party and state machinery. The economic regions were substantially enlarged, and consequently reduced in number: in the RSFSR twenty-four replaced the sixty-seven which still survived in 1962 of the original seventy, and in the Ukraine the number was reduced to seven. The four republics of central Asia were amalgamated into one economic area, and the same amalgamation was scheduled for the three Trans-Caucasian republics and probably for the three Baltic republics. The new regions certainly corresponded more closely to economic realities than had the original 105. Moreover, to ensure co-ordination between regions of widely diversified types of production eighteen intermediate economic regional councils were also set up (these in fact dated from some time earlier).

An elaborate new planning and supervisory mechanism was also created at the centre, under the All-Union Council of Ministers. At the apex of the machinery was the Supreme Council of National Economy (SCNE), whose chairman was a first deputy chairman of the Council of Ministers. Intended to be a general directing and supervisory organ over the entire planning and control mechanism, its legal powers were on paper virtually unlimited: within the sphere of its competence, which was 'the direction of industry and construction throughout the country', it could issue instructions which were 'binding on all state organs irrespective of their subordination'.

Below the Supreme Council of National Economy were three further central organs: the State Planning Committee, or *Gosplan*; the State Committee for Construction, or *Gosstroi*; and the Council of National Economy of the USSR (*Sovnarkhoz* SSSR). These four organs together formed a powerful complex for the planning and control of industry. The three bodies immediately subordinate to the Supreme Council of National Economy had Union-republican status. This meant that they could directly issue orders to their counterparts in the republics; and furthermore that the Councils of National Economy were since the last reform subordinated to both the republican and the All-Union Councils of Ministers, and not, as hitherto, only to the republican Councils of Ministers. On the other hand, the sphere of their competence was increased to the extent that local industries under republican control, which formerly remained outside the competence of the Councils of National Economy and were under the immediate control of the executive committees of the regional (*oblast*) soviets, were now put under the Councils of National Economy.

Finally, the remaining All-Union industrial ministries were transformed into State Committees and new State Committees were created. The object of this reform was stated to be to ensure a more streamlined co-ordination of all technical research and general industrial and scientific policy planning. The numerous committees (there were nearly forty by April 1963) were no longer, as formerly, all subordinated or 'attached' to the All-Union Council of Ministers: one group, which included the State Committees concerned with industries closely connected with matters of defence, was subordinated directly to the Supreme Council of National Economy; another group, comprising the main civilian industries, was subordinated to *Gosplan*; a few committees directly concerned with construction were subordinated to *Gosstroi*, and a few (such as fishery, trade, agricultural machinery) to the USSR Council of National Economy. The powers of the State Committees were enlarged so as to enable each of them to co-ordinate technical research in the entire country within its sphere of interest.

It was claimed for this reorganisation that it will better embody the basic principle of 'democratic centralism', which means the harmonisation of both effective central control and co-ordination, and local initiative. Soviet experience hitherto has shown that the attempt to harmonise these two apparently irreconcilable aims usually results in the failure of one or other of them.

The new system, as reorganised in 1963, did not last long enough for any assessment of it to be possible. Moreover, it clearly met with powerful opposition from the planners, and possibly with sabotage, and its unpopularity was one of the reasons which led to the downfall of Khrushchev in October 1964.

However, some idea of the way it was intended to function can be gleaned from an examination of the way in which *Gosplan* and the USSR Council of National Economy were intended to function, as described by their respective chairmen. *Gosplan* was responsible for all planning, both long term and current. The drawing up of plans was envisaged in three stages. In the first stage *Gosplan*, on the basis of party and state directives and in co-operation with the republics, the USSR Council of National Economy and appropriate state committees and ministries, lays down the 'basic trends of development of the economy of the USSR' for the period embraced by the Plan. At the second stage (the 'democratic' stage) enterprises, the agricultural production administrations, the Councils of National Economy and finally the Union republics draft their plans. At the third stage the national plan is drawn up by *Gosplan* on the basis of this material, with the aid of the State Committees which are subordinate to it. It was, of course, at this stage to be under the general control of its superior, the Supreme Council of National Economy, which in turn was subordinated to the apex, the Council of Ministers—which in practice means the highest officials of party and state so long as the offices of chairman of the Council of Ministers and First Secretary of the Party were combined in one person; and so long as the effective element of the Council of Ministers, its Praesidium, in practice consists of the leading members of the Praesidium of the Central Committee of the Party.

The USSR Council of National Economy was charged with 'implementing' the national plan. The fact that it was a Union republican body was designed to give it the necessary authority. Its prime purpose was to impose central control in those spheres where for lack of specialisation of effort or because of failure of effort the regional councils were unable to ensure efficiency of production. It would thus not only strive to eliminate shortcomings which it was believed only centralisation can achieve but would also attempt to counteract tendencies towards 'localism'.

The working of this system in practice depended on the supremacy of the party apparatus at all crucial points—at the local level, for example, within each economic region, the centralised party network had the task of maintaining centralisation of policy against any tendencies towards 'localism'. Similarly, at the centre, the elaborate machinery for the planning and control of industry could only function, in the absence of central ministries, with the aid of the centralised and all-pervading network of the party machine. Since 15 October 1964 the position is changed, in the sense that the intimate fusion of party and state machinery which Khrushchev sought to achieve has been swept away. The offices of Chairman of the All-Union Council of Ministers and of First (or General) Secretary of the Party were divided between two men, and at the time of writing (June 1970) it is not possible to predict with certainty that this division is going to end, as did that of 1953, in the complete ascendancy of the party side of the partnership. In the course of 1965 a number of reforms of the central government took place. The abolition of the Supreme Council of National Economy was perhaps of political rather than administrative significance. Set up early in 1963 against the wishes of Khrushchev, as it would seem (he had made no reference to this super-planning body when he had outlined his plans for party and government reform in November 1962), the SCNE had played a somewhat obscure part. It was probably of more significance in practice than might have appeared from the reticence with which it was treated in public utterances. But it was also primarily a device by the government planners to counterbalance the ascendancy of the First Secretary, and hence its reason for existence came to an end with his eclipse.

The main change in the machinery of central government effected in 1965 was the abolition of the Councils of National Economy and of the system of regional administration of industry; and the setting up once again of a large number of both All-Union and Union-republican ministries, each responsible for the running of a branch of national economy. (See Appendix.) In one sense this was a return to the traditional Soviet system of administering each branch of the nationalised economy through one central ministry responsible for it in the country as a whole, either directly, or in co-operation with the Union republics. But it would be wrong to view this reform as a complete return to the over-centralised system of administration of the economy which prevailed until 1957. The new leaders embarked at the same time experimentally on a system of decentralisation down to enterprise level, which had been much advocated by a number of leading economists for some years before 1965. This entailed giving individual enterprises limited powers, within the general directives of the national plan and national allocation of resources, of determining their own production on the basis of demand; and of basing the material rewards of such enterprises on efficiency and results, and not on the fulfilment of a detailed plan of production laid down from the centre. By June 1966 this experiment had made a small start and by March 1968 it had been extended to one-third of all enterprises, but it was too early to foretell whether it would solve the difficulties which are inherent in the attempt to plan a complicated consumer economy from the centre. But it was plain that potentially this reform could prove of the utmost import- ance for the economy of the country. The eighteen super-regions have also been retained for purposes of regional economic planning.

The machinery described above is not directly concerned with agriculture, though it is indirectly concerned with maintaining efficient agricultural production on which industry depends, with the determination of the ratio of capital investment in agriculture and with the production of agricultural machinery and of chemi- cal fertilisers. The administration of agriculture at the local level was also reformed in the course of 1962 and 1963. The main pur- pose of the reform was to circumscribe both the administrative district (*raion*) in rural areas and the corresponding rural district party committee, both of which were until March 1962 the main organs for the control over agriculture. The rural districts were approximately halved in number and doubled in size (see chapter 5 for further details). New organisations, known as Collective and State Farm (*Kolkhoz-sovkhoz*) Production Directorates, were set up in the areas of the enlarged rural districts. These Directorates were joint state and party organs, of which a party committee formed an integral part. The decree of 24 March 1962, which reorganised agricultural administration, carried the principle of joint state and party control to the higher levels. The Minister of Agriculture at Union and republican levels was now to be con- cerned solely with questions of research and scientific investiga- tion. For the co-ordination of and control over the work of the Collective and State Farm Production Directorates (which are appointed bodies, including local party, state and farm officials), a hierarchy of Committees for Agriculture was set up at regional (*oblast*), republican, and All-Union levels. At the All-Union level the Committee is headed by a deputy chairman of the Council of Ministers of the USSR; and includes both party officials from the Central Committee apparatus, and state officials—including the Minister of Agriculture, the chairman of the State Committee of

Procurement, a deputy chairman of *Gosplan* and deputy chairmen of other relevant State Committees. The elimination of the hitherto authoritarian party and Soviet district (*raion*) organisations obviously gave rise to considerable opposition, and the whole structure of agricultural control remained in the state of change and uncertainty to which it has always been subject in the USSR. (As N. S. Khrushchev told the Central Committee in March 1962, in spite of 'more than enough' institutions for the administration of agricultural production effective leadership 'essentially has not existed during all the years of Soviet power'.)

Since the fall of Khrushchev the *raion* party committees have been restored, and once again made responsible for the party aspects of control over agriculture. But at the same time the government side of the administration of agriculture was strengthened: in particular, the Ministry of Agriculture, which became a Union-republican ministry, recovered its original powers of overall direction over agriculture. A new Model Statute, on which the rights and powers of the collective farms are based, was published in November 1969. It does not differ very substantially from the old.

There remains to be considered, as an important aspect of Soviet central government, the question of administrative personnel. Since public ownership is universal in industry and in that sector of agriculture which is administered through state farms (as distinct from collective farms) it follows that the category of state employee is a very large one. Soviet law, however, draws a clear distinction between the generic category 'state employee', which includes the whole range from a minister to the humblest manual worker, and the smaller number within this category who are described as 'holders of office'. The distinction in law rests on the fact that the holder of office has the power to perform acts which bring into existence, or effect changes in, or put an end to, juridical relations. This category is much wider than say the higher ranks of the civil service in England, since it includes not only the administrators in a government department, but managers of factories, judges, procurators, book-keepers, higher local government officers, etc. But it is convenient to examine it as the nearest equivalent to a civil service in the English sense of the term.

There are two main reasons why the conception of a civil service, with its own uniform rules, discipline, methods of recruitment, independence and tradition is alien to Soviet political practice. The first is the fact that Soviet authorities have been long accustomed to free disposal over the entire manpower of the country in a constant endeavour to utilise in the interests of political control as well as efficiency the, often very inadequate, available human resources. Secondly, the party has over many years endeavoured to work out a system for the administration of industry which leaves no room for anything in the nature of an independent civil service. Thus, the minister at the head of an All-Union industrial government department is put in sole charge of the branch of industry for which he is responsible: if he fails he will be dismissed, if he succeeds he will reap high rewards. His ministry is the apex of a whole industrial complex, radiating throughout the country: a far-flung network spreads downwards to the individual factories through a series of Chief Administrations and Trusts, or Combines of Trusts, with intermediate stages in some cases. Among his important responsibilities, which he exercises jointly with the appropriate department of the party Secretariat, is the selection of all personnel—administrative, executive, clerical, technical and manual. (At lower levels there is a corresponding sharing of responsibility for appointments between party and administrative heads.) It may be that the experimental system of decentralisation of responsibilities to individual enterprises will eventually result in changes in this traditionally highly centralised system of government and administration. But the principle of the minister as sole master in his own house, subject always to party control, survives, and any minister still has overall responsibility for the selection of personnel. The chairman of a State Committee is in the same position. The right to participate in the appointment of personnel depends on a series of documents to which the term *nomenklatura* applies. These set out the appointments to be filled and the particular officials at different levels, both party and state, who are entitled to be consulted and to decide on the appointments listed. These lists cover virtually all responsible appointments in the country. Nothing is known of the method in use for solving any cases of conflict in the selection of personnel. It is fairly certain that the weight of the party decision will tend to predominate in most cases; and that the normal method of solving conflict would be an appeal to the next highest party instance.

Soviet writers on government lay great stress on the importance of the 'collegium', which is set up in all ministries and in the new parallel organisations. The collegium is appointed by the minister, subject to approval by the Council of Ministers. It usually consists of himself as chairman, his deputies, the principal heads of departments and some other persons. It is advisory only and cannot bind the minister or chairman, who remains solely responsible for his decisions. The collegium exists for discussion of the minister's policy, and it can also organise large meetings to which experienced technical and other persons are invited. Although the collegium cannot enforce its views on the minister, it has the power of appeal against his decision to the Council of Ministers.

The description of the administrative personnel within a ministry or State Committee must be confined to the senior personnel who fall into the category of 'holders of office'. At the same time it must be borne in mind that in many, if not most, respects, all state employees, high and low, are subject to the same conditions of recruitment, employment and discipline. With this limitation in mind, the position of the Soviet 'holder of office' must be examined from four aspects: recruitment, training, conditions of employment, and disciplinary and legal liability.

There is no uniform system of recruitment to state service in the Soviet Union, and in general the practice is governed by numerous legislative enactments, which vary from one branch of the service to another. In general, each head of service recruits his own senior staff in conjunction with the appropriate party authority. At the highest level, that of a Union ministry, for example, the minister will be responsible for recruitment in co-operation with the department of the central party Secretariat in whose competence the particular ministry falls. Certain principles are established as basic to all recruitment. One is that officials must be recruited with due regard to their political and practical or professional qualifications—in that order. By the former is meant a sufficiency of education in and loyalty to party policy and discipline, and it falls naturally to the party authorities to decide on this question. On the practical qualification the head of the relevant service has a large say, though again he is circumscribed either by general enactments relating to all state service or by special enactments relating to particular services—the procuracy, for example, or the State Security service (KGB). The general enactments are contained not only in legislation, but in various directives of the State Committee of the Council of Ministers of the USSR on Labour and Wages which generally co-ordinates problems of employment and earnings. Among the matters stressed in many of the general enactments on recruitment is prohibition of any discrimination on the grounds of ethnic origin or sex. In practice the individual's means of redress are limited to complaints through party or government channels—he has no means of legal redress, and in particular no means of overcoming a decision of the party authorities that his 'political' qualification is unsatisfactory.

Another matter on which many legal enactments exist is the question of the service in the same department of close relatives, which is generally prohibited, though exceptions are permitted.

Since there is no uniform civil service in the Soviet Union, any form of general training of higher administrators, on the French model, for example, is inappropriate. But in recent years more attention has been paid to the systematic training of the different types of specialists. A number of special schools have been set up, and periods of training introduced. The state administrators with whom we are now concerned are invariably recruited either from universities or from higher educational institutions of university or quasi-university status. Some of the latter are attached to and supervised by particular ministries or services, and their graduates, if otherwise satisfactory, will usually find employment in the branch of production or service with which the ministry is concerned. Graduates of other higher educational establishments will be selected when approaching graduation by the ministries or departments for which their qualifications are appropriate, and in practice considerable party and social pressure is exercised to encourage them to accept the posts offered even when no powers of legal direction exist.

Little detailed information is available on conditions of service of the higher state officials, but there is enough available to show that they enjoy a privileged position. The Soviet higher civil service administrator works under conditions of the strictest discipline, and penalties for default and failure are severe, as appears below. But rewards are correspondingly high. Salaries and pensions are relatively high, and appointments of responsibility carry with them the privileges enjoyed by the Soviet élite as a whole—honours and distinctions, priority access to scarce commodities and housing, and to recreational and holiday facilities.

The enjoyment of these monetary and material privileges is however subject to constant review and control by various organs— the State Committee already referred to, the Ministry of Finance, the general organs of control described below (see chapter 8) and, of course, the party. In recent years there has been a general tendency towards the reversal of the enormous inequality of financial rewards which grew up in the course of Stalin's reign, and the administrators have been among those affected by it. In particular there has been a tightening of control in two respects: the proliferation of staffs has been more strictly controlled; and the scale of the lavish financial bonuses which senior administrators often enjoyed has been curtailed.

The system of legal and disciplinary responsibility applicable to the higher state official is of quite extraordinary severity. Even so, frequent incidents described in the press suggest that it is, or was until recently, often possible to escape detection for very long periods. The system of controls to which a state official, classified as 'holder of an office', may be subjected is varied and multiple. In addition to the supervision within his own department or institution, he is subjected to checks of varying frequency by the Ministry of Finance, the procurators, the party and the various Commissions or Committees of Control which have existed under different names at all periods of Soviet history.

The Union-Republican Ministry of Finance is generally responsible for establishments. Through its Establishments Department it maintains a constant check on existing appointments, salaries and the like, and can, or should, prevent any excessive enlargement of establishments in the administration throughout the country.

The responsibility of state officials is a highly complex branch of Soviet law and is contained in numerous enactments, many of them of special application to particular branches of service. Very broadly, the analysis which is contained in the leading textbooks on the subject can be subsumed under three heads: disciplinary responsibility, surcharge and criminal responsibility.

Disciplinary penalties can be imposed both by those who stand above the official concerned in the particular hierarchy, and by party and state organs of control. The penalties imposed generally consist of a reprimand of varying degrees of severity, reduction in rank or dismissal. There is in every case a right of appeal, but only to the next authority in the hierarchy—a penalty imposed by a minister, for example, can be appealed to the Council of Ministers. The decision on appeal is final. There are however provisions, in the case of reprimands, for the entry on the official's record to be removed after a certain period of impeccable service following the reprimand.

Where one of the methods of control reveals that an official has caused material damage by his neglect, his salary can be sur-charged in respect of it. The total amount which can be sur-charged is limited to the equivalent of three months' salary, and the amount deducted in respect of the penalty imposed may not exceed 20% of any one month's salary. Finally, the Criminal Codes contain more or less clearly defined cases of offences which can be committed only by 'holders of office'—such as abuse of official power, or grave failure to perform his official duty. Need-less to say all state officials, like all other officials, are universally liable in respect of ordinary breaches of the criminal law, such as embezzlement or fraud.

The Committee of Party and State Control, set up in November 1962, was given very considerable powers which relate in particu-lar to the highest category of administrators, the 'holders of office'. The Committee, and its subordinate organisations through-out the country, could do all of the following: put a stop to any action of such an official which could cause harm to the interests of the state; lay down a time limit within which an action of which they disapprove must be put right; impose a monetary surcharge on an individual official who in their view has caused financial loss to the state; reprimand, demote or dismiss an official; forward the papers to the procurators for the question of a criminal prosecu-tion to be considered. There is no indication in the decree setting out the powers of this Committee of any right of appeal by the individual. Presumably he had a right of appeal from the particu-lar organ of the State Committee which imposes the penalty to the next in the hierarchy. Also, if a criminal prosecution should result, he had the usual rights enjoyed under the provisions of the Code of Criminal Procedure. (For further details on this Com-mittee see chapter 3.) The People's Control Committee which replaced it in December 1965 has apparently been given similar powers. But it was made clear when this new committee was set up that its powers did not extend to checking on party organs.

7

REPUBLICAN AND LOCAL GOVERNMENT

The administrative divisions of the country have already been sketched in outline. For practical purposes it is convenient to divide the study of the government structure of the various entities into the Union republics and the rest. This corresponds of course to the legally federal structure of the country. It is also in accordance with the hierarchical principle which underlies Soviet administration, according to which the government of every administrative unit is subject both to local control and to control by the unit standing next in the administrative ladder. In this sense both the autonomous republics and the autonomous regions fall under the jurisdiction of one of the five republics in whose territories they are to be found—that of the RSFSR, Uzbekistan, Georgia, Azerbaidjan and Tadjikistan. An autonomous republic has its own Constitution. But this must be consistent with the Constitution of the Union republic of which it forms part, and requires confirmation by the Union republic. Moreover, Union-republican law is binding on the autonomous republic and prevails, in case of conflict, over local legislation. The appropriate Union-republican Council of Ministers can also set aside the orders and decrees of a Council of Ministers of an autonomous republic. (See, for example, articles 19(b), 20, 21 and 46 of the Constitution of the RSFSR.) The autonomous region has no separate Constitution. It comes into existence on the initiative of the Union republic concerned (see, for example, article 19(c) and (d) of the RSFSR Constitution). The Council of Ministers of the Union republic can set aside decisions of the executive committees of the Soviets of autonomous regions (article 46 of the RSFSR Constitution).

It has already been suggested in the discussion of the constitutional structure of the USSR that the juridical federal pattern is inadequate for the understanding of the nature of Soviet government. In the first place, much of the vital administration of the country must perforce cut across the boundaries of the Union republics, if only because these boundaries are dictated by ethnic and historical causes, and have resulted in territories very unequal in size and resources. The inadequacy of the republic as an economic unit for the purpose of planning and industrial control is apparent clearly enough in the pattern of economic regions which was superimposed on the republics in 1957. And secondly, whatever the provisions of the Constitution may lay down, in practice the Union republics enjoy no inalienable rights which cannot be infringed by the All-Union government when it is considered necessary. Its powers (under article 14 of the Constitution, especially) are sufficiently wide to justify virtually any interference with republican activity. Moreover, even where these wide powers may in strict law have been exceeded, the Union republics, in the absence of any judicial instance to which they can appeal to test the validity of All-Union legislative or administrative acts which may infringe republican constitutional rights, are left to such redress as they can exercise through their representation in the All-Union government—in the All-Union Supreme Soviet and in the Council of Ministers. The result has been that over the years the degree of actual autonomy enjoyed by the Union republics has depended on decisions emanating from the All-Union government. It is this circumstance which explains the apparent paradox that in the Soviet Union, alone of all federal governments, the generally observable trend towards the growth of the power of the central government has in the past decade been reversed. In most federal systems the federal government has advanced its power step by step against the entrenched resistance of the component states, cantons or provinces, which have fought for their rights with all the means at their disposal, sometimes with success. No such process has taken place in the Soviet Union. Here the overwhelming power enjoyed both by the party and the government at the centre made possible nearly complete centralisation of all control in Moscow. But this in turn gave rise to considerable administrative congestion and inefficiency, as well as to dissatisfaction in the Union republics. Hence, beginning in 1954, there has been a gradual extension of the powers and responsibilities of the republican governments. By no means all the powers won since 1954 have to date proved permanent. But there is no doubt that republican government is still more of a reality than it was in 1953.

Before examining the changes since 1954, however, it is convenient to look at the federal structure of republican government. The constitutions of the fifteen republics are broadly similar, and to a considerable extent actually identical, and it is therefore sufficient to look at the pattern of the Constitution of the RSFSR, which itself in turn very closely follows that of the USSR. (The reader is also referred to chapter 4 above, where the constitutional power of the All-Union government in relation to the republic is described.) It will, however, be recalled that the Constitution of the USSR does provide for representation of the Union republics in the central government—their chairmen are members of the Praesidium of the Supreme Soviet, and the chairmen of their Councils of Ministers are (at any rate formally) members of the All-Union Council of Ministers. They are of course also represented in the Council of Nationalities of the Supreme Soviet by delegates, but what was more important in practical terms was the existence from 1957 in this chamber of an economic commission; this consisted of a chairman and two commissioners for each Union republic, and provided an informal forum in which the economic interests of the republics could at any rate be urged on the central authorities at the preparatory stage of legislation.

After reciting the general principles of social structure in its first chapter, the RSFSR Constitution deals in its second chapter with state structure. This safeguards the fundamental legal rights of the republic—the right of free secession (article 15) and full residuary sovereign rights, except in so far as limited by article 14 of the Constitution of the Union (article 13 of the RSFSR Constitution). The value of these rights has already been discussed above, as well as (articles 16(a) and 16(b)) the meaning of the republic's rights to conduct its own foreign relations and to maintain its own armed forces. (See chapter 4.) This chapter also confers on the republic the right to determine its own administrative structure, including that of the autonomous republics and regions. This right was until 11 February 1957 vested in the Union government, but by an amendment of the Union Constitution of that date the right of the

Union government in this respect was confined to confirmation of such administrative changes made by the Union republics. Articles 23 and 29, which laid down the administrative subdivisions of some of the Union republics, were at the same time repealed.

The main legal powers of the RSFSR are recited in article 19 of its Constitution. In general, these powers dovetail with those of the Union as set out in article 14 of the Union Constitution and the two articles must be read in conjunction. Thus, for example, the RSFSR confirms its own economic plan and state budget (article 19(h)), but this is limited by the fact that the Union has the duty (under article 14 of its Constitution) to lay down economic plans for the whole country and to enact one single All-Union budget. Again, under article 19(j) of its Constitution the RSFSR determines local taxes—but again this power is expressly limited by the words 'in accordance with the legislation of the USSR'. Again, the republic is given by article 19 the power of legislation in many branches of civil and criminal law, but this too is subject to the overall power of the Union government (under article 14 of the USSR Constitution) to lay down the 'basic principles' of such legislation to which the republics must conform in their legislation: in case of conflict it is the Union law which, under the terms of both constitutions, prevails. The operation of this complex dovetailing has already been discussed in outline in relation to planning and to the control over industry (see chapter 6). The interrelation of the various authorities in the preparation of the national budget and in the sphere of taxation will be discussed below.

Chs. III and IV of the RSFSR Constitution deal respectively with the legislative and executive organs of the republic. The RSFSR Supreme Soviet, which is unicameral, is elected for four years on the basis of one deputy for 150,000 inhabitants. Its regular sessions must take place twice a year. Its Praesidium consists of a chairman, sixteen deputy chairmen (who are in practice the chairmen of the Praesidia of the Supreme Soviets of the sixteen autonomous republics which exist within the RSFSR), fourteen other members and a secretary. The functions, rights and duties of the Praesidium and the Supreme Soviet of the RSFSR are similar to those of the Praesidium and the Supreme Soviet of the USSR—within the sphere of their competence.

The republican Council of Ministers, like its All-Union counterspart, is appointed by the republican Supreme Soviet and it-composition and powers are in principle basically similar. Thus, it consists of a chairman, deputy chairmen, of ministers and of chairmen of State Committees. Its legal competence is also similar in the sense that it is only empowered to issue decrees in implementation of existing legislation, though, as at the All-Union level, this provision is not always observed in practice. Like its All-Union counterpart, it seldom if ever meets as a body, and acts either through its Praesidium of senior ministers without portfolio or through *ad hoc* sub-committees. There are, however, two basic differences between the All-Union and republican Councils of Ministers, which arise from the levels of their competence. First, whereas the All-Union Council of Ministers consists of All-Union and of central Union republican ministers or chairmen of State Committees, the republican Council of Ministers consists of local Union republican and republican ministers and chairmen of committees: as already noted, a Union-republican minister in a republic is subordinate jointly both to the republican and the All-Union Councils of Ministers, the republican ministry (or State Committee) legally only to the former.

The division of ministries and State Committees into these categories of All-Union, Union-republican and republican determines to a large degree the extent of competence allowed to the republics and has varied at different periods. The republican Councils of Ministers were also after 1957 responsible for setting up the Councils of National Economy (*Sovnarkhozy*) of the economic regions within their area: these Councils of National Economy were in 1957 made subordinate only to the republican Councils of Ministers: after 1963 they were placed on a Union republican basis and made jointly responsible at both levels to the relevant Council of Ministers; they were abolished in 1965.

The second main difference which distinguishes the republican from the All-Union Council of Ministers lies in its power of control over subordinate organs. In general the All-Union Council of Ministers can only set aside decrees and orders of republican Councils of Ministers, and then only (in theory at any rate) within the spheres of competence of the Union Government under Article 14. The republican Council of Ministers can set aside decisions and orders of all the following: executive committees (*ispolkomy*) of the Soviets of the areas and regions, including autonomous regions; of the area and regional Soviets, again including autonomous regions; and of the Councils of Ministers of autonomous republics (RSFSR Constitution, article 46).

Chs. V to VIII of the RSFSR Constitution deal with the government organs of all the administrative areas below the Union republic, thus embodying the constitutional framework of Soviet local government. To this it will be necessary to return below. Chs. X, XI and XII deal respectively with the courts, fundamental rights and duties of citizens, and elections. Their provisions are in general so similar in principle to those contained in the All-Union Constitution that they do not call for separate treatment.

Before discussing local government at subordinate levels, it is convenient to consider in more general terms the extent of autonomy in fact at present enjoyed by the Union republics. Here the first question must be that of finance, since no political autonomy can exist where there is no financial autonomy. Article 14(k) of its Constitution empowers the Union government to determine both the taxes to be levied and the income which is to be allocated to republican and local budgets. In practice the republics derive their revenue from two sources: first from a fixed percentage of income from enterprises under republican control, which they are allowed to retain, and secondly by an allocation, which usually takes the form of permission to deduct at source, of a fixed proportion (at present 50%) of direct national taxes, such as income tax. In addition, there are certain minor taxes and dues which the republic determines and levies itself, or allows subordinate administrative units within its territory to levy and spend. Since the new Budget Law of 30 October 1959 it is the republic, and not the Union, which has the power to determine the allocation of reserves to the subordinate units within the territory of the republic. The amount of the allocation to the republican budgets is, of course, one index of the amount of autonomy which the republics are at any one moment being allowed to enjoy. Thus, for example, in 1956 this allocation was nearly one quarter of the total revenue, by 1958 it had grown to a half.

Although, as required by the Constitution, there is only one national budget which is authoritative, the preparation of this document is preceded by the preparation of local budgets, which in turn are embodied in the republican budgets. The republican budget is prepared by the republican Council of Ministers, and approved by the republican Supreme Soviet (RSFSR Constitution, article 103). Similar budgets are prepared at all levels down to the district (*raion*)—there were some 60,000 budgets for the whole of the USSR in 1958, but the number has been somewhat reduced as the result of the reduction in the number of districts. It is, of course, obvious that no local budget, whether district, regional or republican, can be finalised for legal enactment until it has been approved at the Union level and co-ordinated with the Union budget, which is the only authoritative one.

Although the republics cannot therefore be said to enjoy any real autonomy in the matter of finance, they have been given some slightly greater freedom in this respect by the Budget Law of 30 October 1959. Thus they have for the first time been given some discretion in setting off gains against losses, or savings against overspending, in respect of different heads of expenditure in any one year. Again, they have been given the right to decide how they spend any surplus revenue which may be left over at the end of the financial year. These are not great freedoms, but they have tended to make the republics a little more masters in their own house.

The growth of republican autonomy in the budgetary sphere is only part of the general process whereby the republics were allowed greater autonomy in the decade after 1953. This process seemed to reach its height in 1957 and 1958 and may well, in part, have had a political explanation: the need of the First Secretary of the party to win allegiance inside the republics for his new policy of industrial control against his opponents in the party Praesidium at the centre. Indeed, not all of the freedoms won by the republics survived after the First Secretary had weathered the storm—it has already been noted, for example, that the republics lost a considerable degree of autonomy early in 1963 when the Councils of National Economy were placed on the basis of dual subordination, both to the republic and to the Union, and not, as hitherto, solely responsible (in law, at any rate) to the republics (see chapter 6). But several important changes of the period 1954–63 have survived, and should be noted.

The process of extending the area of national life controlled directly and indirectly by the republics began in 1954 with the transfer of industrial enterprises from the immediate control of All-Union ministries to the republics. After the industrial re-organisation of 1957 had been completed it was officially claimed that only 6% of all industry still remained under immediate All-Union control. Very large numbers of enterprises in fact passed to local control: in the RSFSR, for example, it was estimated that

3,400 enterprises, employing 400,000 workers, passed to local control. The authorities entrusted with the immediate control were in 1957 in most cases the regional (*oblast*) Soviets. However, the regions have since 1963 lost control of most of these enterprises, which were placed, along with other industry, under the control of the Councils of National Economy which headed the economic regions. They have not, apparently, regained control over these enterprises since the abolition of the Councils of National Economy.

The important changes in the direction of greater freedom in the sphere of finance have already been noted. Further evidence of the fact that republican government has become more of a reality than it was in the past is provided by the transformation in the past few years of a number of ministries from All-Union to Union-republican status or from Union-republican to republican status. The ministry of justice, for example, is now a republican ministry, with no equivalent at the All-Union level. These are substantial changes, which have undoubtedly conferred a new status on the governments of the republics. They have, among other things, had the effect of giving the representatives of the republics at the centre a much more serious voice in the formulation of decisions. It would, however, be wrong to conclude that the republics are sovereign or autonomous in any real sense of the words, or indeed in the terms proclaimed in their constitutions. The instruments of central control still remain largely unimpaired. The republics have no real means, other than persuasion, of asserting their rights or their claims against the federal power. In the economic field, where the centralised system of planning plays a vital role, the central organs at the All-Union level hold the paramount power.

It is the federal power which in the last resort can determine the budget and the allocation of funds to the republics, though it may well be true that it listens more seriously than in the past to the representations made by the republics. The powerful organs of control such as the procuracy, the State Bank, the Security Service and the Supreme Court (see chapter 8) remain as centralised as before, and have tremendous power which they can exercise directly over all citizens, cutting across the republican authorities. Above all, the Communist Party, which still remains the most effective organ of power in the state, is still completely centralised and can and does intervene at all points in national life, ignoring where it considers it necessary the administrative boundaries of the state structure.

Below the republics come the 'local organs of state power', as the Constitutions describe them. These are the local Soviets—in the areas, regions, the districts, the towns and the rural localities. In all they include in their number a total of 1,820,000 deputies, and they vary in size—the present minimum sizes are 100 deputies for an area or region, 75 for a district, 50 for a town and 25 for a village. Naturally these minima can be and are exceeded— Moscow and Leningrad Soviets number several hundred each. The broad pattern of all these local organs is the same, although their functions and powers vary, and, in general, the laws and regulations governing them are of a quite extraordinary complexity. Each Soviet elects an executive committee (*ispolkom*), which forms the permanent administration for the particular administrative unit. The executive committees are invariably subject to the rule of dual subordination. This means that each executive committee is responsible not only to the Soviet which elects it, but to the executive committee next highest in the hierarchy. Thus a town executive committee will be subordinate to the executive committee of either the district or of the region— depending on its size and importance. This subordination means that the higher executive committee can annul any decision of a lower executive committee. This hierarchy of subordination is one of the causes in practice of delay and red tape, since a decision may, and frequently does, have to go right up the administrative ladder before it becomes final. In the cases of Moscow and Leningrad, however, an exception is permitted under the RSFSR Constitution (article 101): the departments of the executive committees of these two cities are directly subordinate to the appropriate ministries of the RSFSR.

Two features should perhaps be emphasised at the outset. Soviet practice does not regard these local government authorities as in any sense autonomous—they are officially described as local agencies of the central government. By the principle of 'democratic centralism' they partake of a democratic character mainly through participation in decisions affecting them which are taken at a higher level; and through the fact that they are said to be democratically elected. In practice this 'democratic' element is very much vitiated by the degree of party control which is exercised. The party can and does control the elections—the single candidate is as much a feature of local as of central elections. The influence of the party is also preponderant in the executive committees—indeed there are many instances where the local party committee and the executive committee of the local Soviet (or local 'town council') are housed in the same building, and there is never any doubt in Soviet conditions where the real authority lies. The general constant control from above by the party necessarily negates much of the democratic control which is, under the Constitution, vested in the electors. This said, there have been certain trends in the past decade which have made Soviet local government authorities somewhat more democratic, independent and genuine than they were before. The first marked trend has been the increased popular participation in local activities—indeed the reliance on voluntary local service is a characteristic feature of the whole system. The second trend, which is in some measure a consequence of the first, has been the decrease in the size of the paid apparatus of officials. Thirdly, there has been a healthy tendency towards stricter enforcement of observance of the law, and an attempt made to put down the frequent assumption by local authorities of powers which they do not in law possess. Finally there has been some enlargement of the scope of their activities.

The complexity of Soviet local government precludes anything more than a short summary of the main features which characterise the structure and activity of the many authorities which exist. The first feature is the absence of any strict allocation of functions: the same functions fall under the jurisdiction of different authorities at different levels in the hierarchical ladder. Thus all authorities normally have responsibility for budget and planning, which means that they are all called on to contribute their suggestions in these spheres for ultimate co-ordination by the Union republics and then by the All-Union government. Again, practically all authorities have some responsibilities for local trade and industry, transport, housing, agriculture, social insurance, education, health and the maintenance of public order. This general pattern is subject to the qualification that certain subjects generally form the main responsibility of certain levels of authorities. Thus, the district committees (*raiispolkom*) carry the main burden in matters of finance, below the region and the republic. Until 1962 the district was also the main authority for the control of agriculture, but since then the control has passed to joint state and party administrations, and the areas of the districts have been enlarged to correspond to these administrations. Similarly, until 1962, the bulk of local industry was under the control of the regions. Since the end of 1962 only small-scale industry still remains under the control of numerous authorities at all levels. Some of their revenue is in fact derived from such partly local enterprises, though the bulk of it still depends on assignment from above. This multiplicity of authorities in the same branch of activity is undoubtedly a cause of much delay and 'bureaucracy', which is frequently criticised in the press. That the system does not cause even more confusion is due to the hierarchical nature of Soviet local government, which ensures that a decision can always be sought by appeal to a higher level, or by the intervention of the party, or by both methods.

Legally, all authority is vested at each level in the local Soviet. The Soviet meets at comparatively infrequent intervals. Its main duty is stated to be the supervision of the work of its executive committee. In practice the predominance of party control over the executive committees and over the Soviets has hitherto in most cases enabled the executive committees effectively to dominate the Soviets. Great stress is laid in the textbooks and in the press on the activities of the permanent commissions of the local Soviets. These are set up for the main branches of activity dealt with by the executive committee, and consist not only of the deputies of the local Soviet, but of wider sections of the public. (In 1962 there were said to be over 230,000 such commissions distributed among nearly 50,000 local Soviets, composed of over 1,300,000 local deputies and of over 2,300,000 'activists' drawn from the public.) The development of local commissions on this scale is recent, and it seems probable that to a limited extent they contribute to enforcing greater efficiency on the executive committees which they are charged to supervise.

The executive committee is formally elected by the local Soviet, and can technically be overruled by it. Hitherto, the party has been successful in asserting its control over all local elections to a very considerable extent. The executive committee maintains a permanent staff and an office and is in fact the executive authority for the locality. Its departments are prescribed in the republican constitution. Every executive committee has certain legal powers to enforce its orders, including wide powers of inflicting fines in a

summary administrative manner. Another fairly recent development has been the setting up of commissions attached to the
executive committees for certain specific supervisory tasks. Thus,
'administrative commissions' attached to executive committees of
local authorities are charged with the duty of ensuring observance
of law and with the infliction of minor administrative penalties.
They too consist both of deputies and of members of the public.
Certain provisions for appeal against their decisions are usually
laid down. Of especial interest, perhaps, are the 'supervisory
commissions' which have been set up in recent years by executive
committees of the larger town and regional authorities (in the
RSFSR, for example, since 24 May 1957). These commissions are
charged with the duty of supervising the observance of the law
in the penal corrective labour institutions, and with the re-educa-
tion of the inmates. They are 'set up' (not elected) by the executive
committee, and include representatives not only of the Soviet, but
of trade unions, of those engaged in the administration of health
and education, and of the Communist youth organisation
(*Komsomol*). They work under the direction of the executive
committee and have powers to inspect and to make representations.

There are also various other forms of 'mass' participation in the
work of local authorities. It is probably true that this drawing of
the public into the work of local authorities satisfies one aspect of
the principle of democratic centralism; namely participation on a
wide scale by the public (always under party guidance) in the work
of government. It is unlikely that the central government authorities or the party authorities could relax the other aspect of
'democratic centralism', namely central control, to the extent of
allowing even limited decision-making to these mass organs. To
do so would be a departure from a form of government which has
become a deeply rooted party tradition—government from the top.
But the trend in recent years towards greater participation by the
public may at any rate ensure that the decisions which are handed
down from the top do at least take account to a somewhat greater
extent than hitherto of the interests and wishes of the governed.

Deputies of local Soviets are unpaid, but must be released for
duty without loss of wages. They are expected to, and within the
limits open to them probably do, look after the interests of their
constituents. One of their rights is to address written questions to
the executive committee and its officials and to receive an answer.

The effectiveness of this weapon varies at different times. The nature of party control is such that it can easily, if it wishes, make it too personally dangerous for a local deputy to risk his whole future on awkward questions. But there are times when the party authorities at the top appear to encourage the most searching criticism and discussion. Some take advantage of this liberty to do their duty. Others, more circumspect, prefer to play for safety. The difficulty of life in the Soviet Union is that one can never in practice know with certainty the limits within which at any particular moment criticism can be regarded as safe.

8

THE ORGANS OF CONTROL

The Soviet system of government is characterised by the existence of a multiplicity of organs and institutions for checking, supervision and control over the activities of the entire machinery of administration. First in importance among such organs is, of course, the party, whose role in this respect has already been discussed. But the party, while exercising supervision, can itself be an object of supervision. In general, a party organ (though not, in theory, at any rate, party members in their ordinary capacity as citizens) is exempt from supervision by anything other than the organs of the party itself superior to itself. The procurators, for example, cannot extend their supervision to any party committee or secretariat. The Party-State Control Committee, when it was set up in 1963, was originally intended to include the organs and officials of the party in its area of supervision. However it soon became plain that, whatever the original intention, this Committee was not in practice allowed to discipline members of the party apparatus directly, but only to refer their cases for enquiry and disciplinary action, if required, to the appropriate party instance. Since the replacement of the Party-State Control Committee by the People's Control Committee in December 1965, it has been made clear that its jurisdiction does not extend to organs of the party. In the discussion of the various organs of control and supervision which follows below, one overall consideration must be borne in mind. The members of all these institutions are not only frequently party members (in some cases, such as that of the State Security Service, invariably party members) but are subject to direct control by the party, through one of the departments of the central Secretariat. Therefore, in every case, behind the activity of the particular organ or instrument of control—security services, procurators or the State Bank for example—there lies the continuous and ever present guiding hand and authority of the party organs.

The significance of this party control for the balance of power in the state becomes particularly apparent when one examines the State Security Service. This service, which in one form or another has existed since the earliest period of Soviet rule, has undergone many formal changes, of which lack of space precludes any description. It may however be convenient to list, for identification purposes, the various initials by which the Security Service has been known in the course of Soviet history: CHEKA, VECHEKA, GPU, OGPU, NKVD, NKGB, MVD, MGB, KGB. The present symbol, KGB, dates from 1954, and represents the words: Committee for State Security. This committee is attached to the All-Union Council of Ministers, but there are similar committees at republican, regional and other local levels. The system is completely centralised, in the sense that it is hierarchically directed by its chairman at the All-Union level, and in the further sense that the Union republics have little if any autonomy in this sphere.

In the later years of Stalin's regime the security organs acquired a power and an autonomy, under Stalin's direct control, which made them the main instrument of his personal rule of terror. Nominally (until 1951) under the Ministry of Interior, the security organs were in fact directly controlled by Stalin's personal Secretariat, which was probably identical with the Secret Department of the Secretariat of the Central Committee. They were independent of both party and state control or supervision. Their powers were never fully defined by public enactment, though an enactment of 1934 did give the security organs wide authority to deport to penal camps of confinement persons considered dangerous to the state. There was no appeal from this decision, and indeed the accused had no right to be present at the decision. This limited and publicly declared power was vastly extended by unpublished instructions, which included the use of torture in the course of interrogation and the power of execution by shooting. The periods of detention were in practice repeatedly extended, and between 1929 and 1953 many millions of people were deported and confined in conditions of quite appalling inhumanity or shot.

The reforms after 1953 in the sphere of security, which followed upon the arrest and execution of L. P. Beria (head of the Security Service since 1938), were mainly in three directions. In the first place the special powers of deportation, confinement and execution without trial were repealed. Secondly, the control of the KGB became the regular province of the party organs, in practice exercised by the department of Administrative Organs of the Central Secretariat—so far as is known the secret department or personal Secretariat did not survive Stalin. And thirdly, the powers of the security organs in the conduct of investigations were circumscribed by published laws in place of secret instructions—at any rate, if secret instructions exist, their nature and content have never been discovered. Since, in spite of secrecy, information on these secret instructions did leak out in Stalin's time, it is a fair inference that no such secret instructions are officially in operation now.

These are important limitations. Nevertheless the police and security arm of the Soviet government is a formidable engine. In the first place, the state disposes of considerable armed forces. For the general control of crime and public order there are the forces of the militia. These are under the control of the Union Republican Ministry of the Interior, its Republican counterparts, and their subordinate departments throughout the country. The local administrations responsible for the militia work in close co-operation with the executive committees of the appropriate Soviets. The militia have wide powers for the maintenance of public order, including the power of inflicting fines by administrative decision, and power to detain and to conduct preliminary investigations in many cases of suspected crime.

In addition to the militia, the state disposes of several large bodies of internal troops, fully armed and equipped, for the maintenance of internal order. The most important of these armed security forces are the Border Guards and the Internal Troops. The Border Guards are subordinated to the KGB. The Internal Troops, which number several hundred thousand, may now be subordinated to the All-Union Ministry of Maintenance of Public Order, which was set up in 1966.[1] So long as the Ministries of Maintenance of Public Order were republican only, it is extremely improbable that the internal troops were subordinated to them, since these special highly trained and highly armed security troops have always been maintained under centralised command for rapid use whenever internal emergency should require it. Until the setting up of the union-republican Ministry of Maintenance of Public Order they were most probably subordinated to the KGB and it is not possible to say with certainty that they do not even now remain subordinate to it.

The KGB is the organ responsible both for external espionage and for internal counter-intelligence. It is also responsible for the preliminary investigation of all crimes against the state—from espionage to 'anti-Soviet propaganda'; of such crimes as loss of documents or illegal frontier crossing; and of certain 'economic' crimes. The KGB officials have power to arrest on suspicion, but must notify the procurator within twenty-four hours: the procurator must then either sanction the arrest or order the discharge of the accused. As a general rule, to which there are exceptions, confinement under detention during the investigation of a crime must not exceed two months, but can be extended by order of senior procurators for a further six or even nine months.

As for the conduct of the preliminary investigation, the KGB officials are by law now subject to the same rules as all other investigators. These rules are designed to prevent the use of force and other improper means in order to obtain a confession, and to safeguard the rights of the accused or of the suspect to defend himself against the charge. The responsibility for ensuring the observance of these rules is placed upon the procurators. It is impossible to say whether these rules are always observed in practice, since the absence of an uncontrolled press means that only those cases which the authorities wish to publicise become known. The victim of a breach of the rules has no remedy in the courts, either by way of an application for an order for release, or of redress in damages against the guilty official. The only remedy open to the victim is to complain to the procurator, or to use the less formal channels of complaint, such as the party or the party press. Certainly some cases of redress obtained by these means have been publicised in the past years: reiterated complaints at official conferences and the like of continued violations in practice of the rules designed to protect the individual against an all-powerful state suggest that old habits die hard.

The system of general supervision of legality by a corps of state officials known as procurators is of long standing in Russia. It was originally instituted by Peter the Great in 1722. However, after the reform of the legal system in 1864 the procuracy largely fell into abeyance, and the rights of the individual were left to the protection of the courts and of the law of the land. The system of procurators was revived after the revolution, and in one form or another it has been in existence ever since. The basic structure of the procuracy is laid down by articles 113 to 117 of the 1936 Constitution. The Procurator General of the USSR is charged with the general duty of supervision over the 'meticulous observance of the law by all ministries and institutions subordinate to them as well as by individual holders of office and citizens'. He is appointed by the Supreme Soviet for seven years, and in turn appoints or confirms the appointments of subordinate procurators at all administrative levels from Union republic to districts and towns. The lower procurators are appointed for five years. There is no provision in the Constitution for removal, though such removals have in fact taken place. It will be observed that the system is completely centralised—and indeed the importance of the independence of all procurators from influence by any local organ is laid down in the Constitution, and the need for this centralisation was emphasised by Lenin. The present position of the procuracy is laid down in a statute of the Supreme Soviet of 24 May 1955 and in a further decree of the Praesidium of the Supreme Soviet of 7 April 1956.

Subject to the right of the Praesidium of the Supreme Soviet to set aside his order, the Procurator General is supreme over his entire apparatus and his orders are binding on all its officials. The structure of his central apparatus illustrates the scope of his activities: it includes a department for General Supervision; a Bureau of Investigation for the supervision of the preliminary enquiries (which, in Soviet law, precede indictment and trial in criminal cases) conducted by the militia or by his own investigating officers; a department for the supervision of investigations conducted by the KGB; departments for the supervision respectively of criminal and civil trials in the courts; a department for the supervision of places of confinement; and various departments for statistics, administration and criminological research. The subordinate offices throughout the country are organised on a similar pattern.

The procuracy is a unified service, admission to which must be preceded by six months' probation followed by a year's attachment. It is confined to law graduates (or the equivalent) and, in normal practice, to members of the party.

The duty of general supervision by the procurators is confined to questions of legality—it does not extend to efficiency or expediency, for which other supervisory organs are responsible. It extends to the acts of ministries and their subordinate agencies and enterprises; of executive agencies of local Soviets; of 'co-operatives and other public organisations'; and of all officials and citizens. This list is not in fact as extensive as may at first sight appear. It does not, for example, extend to acts of the Councils of Ministers or of the Supreme Soviets at the All-Union, or republican or autonomous republican, level. Nor does it extend to any organs of the party, since the party is not 'a voluntary organisation', but 'the leading core' of all voluntary and state organisations as stated in article 126 of the Constitution of the USSR. (It did however extend to Councils of National Economy.) Within these limits the duty of general supervision (which has varied in its effectiveness at different periods of Soviet history) is to detect violations of the law; and, once detected, to take measures to stop the violations and, if need be, set in motion the prosecution of the guilty.

The sources of information open to the procurators for the purpose of general supervision include complaints from individuals and information obtained from the agency suspected of violation of the law. For this purpose the procurators are given extensive powers of calling for documents and explanations and for instituting enquiries. When once an illegality has been detected, the procurator can either institute a full enquiry by means of a 'protest' or a 'proposal' (similar but not identical acts) or initiate criminal, civil, administrative or disciplinary proceedings against individual officials or citizens guilty of violations of the law.

The law imposes on the procurator a general obligation to ensure that at all stages of a criminal trial there shall be no violation of the law by anyone whomsoever (see for example article 25 of the Code of Criminal Procedure for the RSFSR). Accordingly, existing legislation imposes very detailed duties on the procurator in this respect. He is responsible from start to finish for the preliminary investigation of every case, whether the investigation be conducted by his own investigating officers, by the militia or by the officials of the KGB. He can reverse the decision, transfer a case from one investigator to another, put an end to the proceedings and release the accused, and issue the necessary directives in the case. Should the accused be indicted for trial, however, it is the procurator who conducts the prosecution. At this stage he is placed in a dual position, since he is both prosecutor and guardian of the rights of the accused. In his first capacity he may, and often does, appeal against an acquittal, or against what he considers to be an inadequate sentence. In his second capacity he may, and again in practice often does, appeal or 'protest' against a decision which he believes to be in violation of the rights of the accused. (The difference between appeal and protest is technical: a protest, as distinct from an appeal, is lodged when the case is not yet closed.)

The procurator has two other main functions relative to the operations of the law and of penal institutions. He is required (though in practice this is not always done) to participate in all civil trials as well as criminal. The purpose of this participation is to assist the court with legal expertise, if required, with regard to matters arising on the investigation of civil proceedings. Procurators are also entrusted with the supervision of places of confinement within their jurisdiction. They are required to visit and inspect them regularly, to interview prisoners and check on their treatment and to order the release of those illegally confined. Their powers in the case of other illegalities which they may discover seem, however, to be confined to lodging a protest 'in accordance with prescribed procedure' (article 33 of the Statute of 24 May 1955).

From the point of view of the individual, his most important right, indeed his only effective right in Soviet practice, is that of lodging a complaint. The procuracy is only one, but a very important, channel for individual complaints. The other important channels are the party, where an act by a party member is involved; and the machinery of the local Soviets, where administrative acts are involved. (The Central Committee of the CPSU on 2 August 1958 issued a directive criticising the treatment of these complaints by administrative bodies, and calling for improvements.) The right of the individual to lodge a complaint with the procurator is very wide in scope, and, on the whole, informal in the matter of procedure. If the complainant has not yet exhausted the normal administrative channels of redress the procurator will usually confine himself to advising him on the correct method of procedure. Otherwise the procurator is required to investigate the complaint, and if necessary to take action to secure redress. Elaborate rules are laid down with regard to the procedure to be followed, so far as the procurator is concerned. As for the complainant, if he fails to secure satisfaction, his only remedy is to complain to the next instance in the procuratorial hierarchy.

It is a characteristic of Soviet constitutional and criminal law that it confers on the citizen a great number of rights but provides virtually no effective means to enforce them. There is nothing corresponding to a writ of *habeas corpus*; and there is in practice virtually no redress possible in the courts against any official— police, state or party—for malpractices other than embezzlement of funds. The supervision exercised by the procurators is therefore a vital safeguard for the accused. There is no doubt that in recent years many procurators have discharged their duties honestly to the benefit of many individuals who would otherwise have been left without any redress whatever. On the other hand it would be idle to conceal the fact that this form of redress is, to say the least, precarious. The procurators, as Soviet writers repeatedly stress, act under general party control and are bound first and foremost to carry out the policy of the party. If the policy of the party requires or endorses illegal action towards an individual the procurator will afford him no protection. In 1961, for example, the procurator successfully appealed against a sentence of the maximum term of imprisonment imposed by the court on a man convicted of an economic offence on the sole ground that the sentence was too mild in view of the fact that, *subsequently* to his conviction, the death penalty was enacted for this kind of offence. Yet this retrospective application of an increased penalty is expressly prohibited by article 6 of the Fundamentals of Criminal Law enacted by the Supreme Soviet on 25 December 1958. Here procurators, judges and the party were all at one to enforce an illegality at the expense of an individual's life. In the last two decades of Stalin's reign the procurators were bound by enactments very similar to the one described above to protect the individual; yet this notoriously did not prevent the repeated commission of the most flagrant illegalities. The improvement in recent years is due less to an improvement in the law than to the tolerance by the party, in the changed climate which has succeeded the death of Stalin, of greater observance of the law.

As a result of a decision of the Plenum of the Central Committee of the CPSU which met in November 1962 a new and powerful organ of overall supervision and control was set up. Known as the Committee of Party and State Control of the Central Committee of the CPSU and of the Council of Ministers of the USSR, it took over, on paper, at all events, the functions of general supervision of party organs and party members hitherto exercised by the Committee of Party Control; and the functions of the state organ of supervision over the performance of their administrative duties by state institutions which had been known at various periods of its recent history as the Ministry, or Committee of State, or Soviet, Control. The structure and functions of the new committee were laid down in a joint directive of the Central Committee of the party and the Council of Ministers of the USSR, of which an official summary was published on 18 January 1963. (The full text was published in 1964.)

The directive stresses that the aim of this new engine of control was not only to check conformity with the law, but also efficiency of action at all levels of administration: it was to aim at prevention as well as at cure, and must do so with the widest possible participation of 'the masses'. The new system envisaged a centralised hierarchy of committees at all levels at the centre of the Union, in republics, in areas and regions, in towns, in districts, in the *kolkhoz/sovkhoz* production administrations and in the zonal industrial administrations. (In areas and regions where, between 1963 and 1965, there were separate party committees and Soviets for industry and for agriculture there were two Committees of Party and State Control.) The committees at all levels were presided over by one of the party secretaries of the party committee at the level concerned, and included representatives of the trade unions, the *Komsomol*, the press, workers, peasants and intellectuals—both full-time and paid, and part-time unpaid. In order to represent 'the masses' in the activity of this hierarchy of committees, 'groups of co-operation' consisting of 'the most active comrades, both party and non-party', were set up in all industrial enterprises, state farms and collective farms and in all communal dwellings. The purpose of the 'groups of co-operation' was to inform the local committee of persons guilty of illegality, inefficiency, dishonesty, unconscientious behaviour and the like.

The Committees of Party and State Control were given very stringent powers. They could carry out investigations into the activities of all party and Soviet organs, all industrial and agricultural enterprises, and of all members of the organs of control and supervision within ministries. They could order defects which they discovered to be put right; and could set aside acts and orders of which they disapproved. They could impose all manner of disciplinary measures on 'holders of office' (but not, apparently, on party officials, who are not covered by this description): they could impose a financial surcharge, they could demote or dismiss; and they could forward the papers to the procurators with a view to a criminal prosecution being launched. There was no provision for appeal by the individuals affected. But it may be assumed that, in accordance with ordinary Soviet practice, it was open to an individual affected to appeal from a lower committee to a higher committee in the hierarchy. The Committee of Party and State Control was, as its name implied, intended to be a joint organ of both party and government. Its Chairman was both a Secretary of the Central Committee and a deputy Chairman of the Council of Ministers of the USSR. As such it was an innovation character-istic of Khrushchev, whose policy it was to encourage fusion of party and government administrative organs, so long as party influence remained predominant. It was therefore only to be expected that this hybrid organisation would be abolished, along with other hybrids of this nature, after Khrushchev's fall. It was replaced in December 1965 by a similar People's Control Com-mittee, but apparently intended to be of somewhat lower status (judging by the status of the new Chairman, who replaced the Chairman of the Committee of Party and State Control, A. N. Shelepin). However its legal powers, which in Soviet conditions are in practice a good deal less important than political status, to seek out malpractices in the administration of the economy, remain the same.

Mention has already been made of the function of the Ministry of Finance in exercising control over establishment matters throughout the entire administration (see chapter 6). Equally, if not more, important is the supervisory function exercised by the State Bank (*Gosbank*), which is known as 'control by the rouble'. The Bank, which is a centralised All-Union organisation, is in a position to exercise a considerable controlling influence over enterprises throughout the Union through its operation of credit. All state enterprises are required to keep their accounts with the State Bank and to make all but the smallest payments through the Bank. The Bank is thus enabled to ensure that all resources are being applied in accordance with the plan or that price and wage rates are in accordance with official regulations covering these matters. It should also be able, except where great ingenuity is exercised, to detect attempts by enterprises to engage in private, illicit deals. The Bank also issues short-term credits for purposes within the orbit of the national plan. Credits are increased or decreased according as the targets laid down by the plan are over- or under-fulfilled by each enterprise. The Bank also plays an important role when an enterprise gets into financial difficulties. In the last resort the Bank can even declare an enterprise insolvent and generally take over, reorganise and manage the bankrupt enterprise.

There are various other methods, other than those described above, by which the government authorities can to a greater or lesser extent exercise effective supervision over activity throughout the country. It may be observed that this problem of effective supervision is far from solved in the view of the Soviet authorities —the setting up in 1962 of a new and ostensibly more potent engine, the Committee of Party and State Control, was explained by the failure of supervision before then to prevent and eradicate inefficiency and illegality. Of course, the vastness of the country, the heritage of exaggerated centralisation over many years, planned shortages, a low standard of living and above all the difficulties which arise in a modern economy, with an increasing consumer demand, if an attempt is made to plan production, prices and distribution from the centre—all contribute to make supervision of the kind which is considered necessary difficult to achieve. There are a number of other institutions which, to a greater or less extent, participate in the process of checking and supervision. The only one which need be mentioned in this context is State Arbitration (*Gosarbitrazh*). This institution is in effect a system of administrative courts, at All-Union, republican and regional levels, as well as in Moscow and in Leningrad, which exists for solving disputes which may arise between state, co-operative organisations (other than collective farms) and other public organisations. These arbitration tribunals apply not only the ordinary law of the land, but other special enactments as well. They are charged with the duty of reporting to the proper authorities any breaches of the law which may come to light in the course of their activity. They are however not supposed to interfere with the management or running of enterprises, and are therefore not strictly a supervisory organ designed to detect inefficiency. In practice the influence of State Arbitration in this sphere is also quite considerable. So many matters relating to production by state enterprises are covered by laws or decrees in the Soviet Union that the border line between inefficiency and illegality is often very difficult to draw, especially since the state leaves very little to the discretion of the individual manager. The State Plan, for example, in its entirety has the force of law. Thus, in ensuring compliance with laws and regulations, State Arbitration is at the same time enforcing the standards and policy for production laid down by the state.

The system of courts of law is governed by ch. IX of the Constitution of the USSR. At the apex of the hierarchy of courts is the Supreme Court of the USSR. There are also Supreme Courts in all Union republics and in each autonomous republic; there are courts in areas, circuits and regions. The lowest level of courts is formed by the People's Courts, which are set up in the towns, and in the urban (municipal) and rural districts (*raion*). All Soviet judges are elected. The judges of the Supreme Courts of the Union and of the Union and autonomous republics are elected by the appropriate Supreme Soviet for five years. Judges of all other courts, apart from the People's Courts, are similarly elected for five years by the appropriate Soviets. The judges of the People's Courts are directly elected by secret ballot in which all adult citizens participate, likewise for five years. There are also certain special courts, of which the most important are the military courts.

The Supreme Court of the USSR consists of a president and a varying number of members, who include the presidents of the republican Supreme Courts *ex officio*. The Supreme Court of the USSR sits either in plenary session or by division, of which there are three: for civil cases, for criminal cases and the military division. The plenary sessions, which must take place at least once every three months, are for the exercise of the appellate and supervisory functions of the Supreme Court. There are five such functions listed in the Statute of 12 February 1957 which governs the Supreme Court: the rehearing of suits and trials dealt with by one of its divisions on the demand or 'protest' of the president of the Supreme Court, or of the Procurator General of the USSR; re-examination of judgments issued by the republican Supreme Courts, following upon a protest by the President of the Supreme Court of the USSR or the Procurator General alleging that the judgment or decision of a republican Supreme Court is in conflict either with All-Union law or with the 'interests' of other republics;

the issuing of general instructions and explanations of the law for the benefit of its own divisions of all inferior courts; assisting the Praesidium of the Supreme Soviet with interpretation of the law; and resolving conflicts between the judicial organs of the Union republics. The jurisdiction of the divisions is both appellate and of first instance—in the latter case the jurisdiction is limited to cases of 'exceptional importance'.

All other courts in the hierarchy of courts have both appellate jurisdiction and jurisdiction at first instance, except for the People's Courts, which only have first-instance jurisdiction. All courts have jurisdiction in both civil and criminal matters, but the extent of the jurisdiction of each level of court varies with its stage in the hierarchy. There is usually free right of appeal from one court to the next highest court, up to the Supreme Court. Legal aid is provided in most cases. Soviet judges are not required to have legal qualifications, though in practice the great majority now have some legal training. They are mostly elected by a system of elections which follows very closely the election of deputies to the Soviets—there is one candidate only, and he invariably secures a virtually unanimous vote. Judges are required to sit together with 'people's assessors' who are chosen from a panel to which they are elected. The assessors are not jurymen—they do not deliberate separately from the judge, and they are not the judges of fact. In practice it is almost unknown for them to disagree with the judge or to overrule his judgment.

According to article 112 of the Constitution, 'judges are independent and subject only to the law'. This rule, which is fundamental to all real administration of justice as distinct from arbitrary executive control, is in Soviet practice limited by four factors, which render it of little effect. First, all judges are subject to disciplinary control—they can be freely reprimanded, recalled, moved or removed for misconduct. Secondly, Soviet theory does not recognise law as superior to party policy. The policy of the party is repeatedly asserted to be supreme, and therefore binding on the judges as on everyone else. This subjection of the judge to party policy is not regarded as an infringement of the judge's independence by Soviet theorists of law, since all law is regarded as an expression of the will of the people, and the party as vanguard of the people can best claim to express that will. (In practice the Central Committee has a special department for Administrative Organs, so called, which is responsible *inter alia* for the control over judges.) Thirdly, while trials must, except where the law provides otherwise, be held in open court (article 111) there is no provision requiring the reporting of all cases by the press. Since the press is controlled by the party and by the state, trials in the courts are reported selectively, and those that are reported in the press are often described very tendentiously. The public therefore, even if it were in Soviet conditions able to do so, is often deprived of the necessary information for exerting pressure in an endeavour to protect the courts. Finally, although this is inconsistent with the basic principles of criminal law enacted in 1958 by the Supreme Soviet, there exist in practice a large number of quasi-tribunals which do not administer law at all, but have stringent powers. These quasi-tribunals include such bodies as public gatherings which are granted the power to exile for up to five years, with confiscation of property, persons who lead a 'parasitical' life. These public gatherings are under the control of the party and provide virtually no safeguard to the individual.

In spite of these serious limitations, it is nevertheless true to say that great improvements have taken place in the Soviet legal system since the death of Stalin. The improvement has been mainly in three directions, so far as the criminal law is concerned. First, the former virtually unlimited powers of the security arm have been considerably curtailed. Secondly, the procedure at trials has been improved, and certain additional safeguards provided for the accused. Thirdly, the procurators, who are charged with defending the rights of the accused, have been discharging their duty with greater zeal than before.

The position today can be fairly summarised as follows, so far as the criminal law is concerned. The law is very severe in many cases—the death penalty is prescribed and regularly inflicted for nearly a dozen offences, many of them of an economic nature, such as bribery or 'speculation'. But the application of the law is, with notable exceptions, much fairer than it was when Stalin was in command. The party can, and on occasions does, interfere with the administration of the law. But it is also true to say that genuine efforts are from time to time made to ensure greater conformity with the law and with legal standards. It can properly be objected that so long as the party retains the power of circumventing or influencing the administration of the law, all law is tolerated law and no more; and 'tolerated law' is not really law at all, since law can only flourish where it exists as of right. This is probably true. But even tolerated law is probably better than no law at all. Moreover, the tradition of legality is slow to develop in every society. There is virtually no such tradition in Soviet society, since the highly developed (if restricted) pre-revolutionary legal tradition was destroyed and rooted out along with the Bench and Bar of Imperial Russia. It may be that a generation of 'tolerated law' will help to lay the foundations for such a future tradition.

1. Renamed Ministry of the Interior in November 1968.

9

RECENT POLITICAL DEVELOPMENTS

Even a casual observer of the Soviet political system, both at the present day and in the course of its history, must immediately be struck by the very high degree of centralised control to which it is, and always has been, subject. Indeed, a moment's reflection will show that there are very good reasons why this should be so. First, there is the ubiquitous party which, not only in terms of Article 126 of the Constitution, but in actual fact is the 'leading core' of all aspects of political, social and industrial life. And the Communist Party is, and always has been, completely centralised, in organisation and in discipline. Second, it is impossible to imagine an economy, controlled by a central all-embracing plan to the extent to which Soviet theory and practice demands, which is not highly centralised. But there is a third reason as well. For generations party and state officials, as well as those who administer the nationalised enterprises and the collective farms have lived under a command system which is exacting and unforgiving. The risks of showing initiative are known from experience to be great; the penalties for error (which in every authoritarian system are invariably visited in the first instance on subordinates) are severe. It is easiest to carry out orders from above—and this is what for generations Soviet party and government officials have preferred. It is only necessary to recall the hornets' nest which Khrushchev stirred up in 1957 when he tried, however crudely, to load more personal responsibility on reluctant managers of enterprises; or again in 1963, when he attempted, however ineptly, to force high party officials to shoulder greater burdens and to show more initiative. It was not for nothing that Lenin expressed surprise very early on in the Soviet régime's existence that such questions as the supply of tins of meat to Moscow should be coming up for decision in the Politburo.

Centralised planning has its advantages, particularly in a vast, multi-national country like the USSR. But it also has obvious dis-advantages: plan fulfilment takes precedence over everything else, for example, to the complete disregard for the interests of the consumer. The shops fill up with goods which remain unsold, while there are shortages of goods which are in real demand. The malfunctioning of the official system has to be adjusted by an, at times, vast unofficial semi-legal black market in goods and services, with consequent corruption and unfairness. Or again, highly centralised allocation of raw materials results in long and wasteful cross-hauls of manufactures through the length and breadth of the country. Khrushchev's economic reform of 1957 was designed to meet these and other drawbacks inherent in centralisation by setting up a number of economic regions, each of which was intended to become a unit responsible for the totality of economic output. As will be recalled, this proved unpopular and unwork-able: the system had to be severely modified during the few years of power that remained to Khrushchev and was dismantled after his fall in 1964.

What looked like a revolutionary new system for the manage-ment of industry, embodying quite a different type of decentral-isation, from that embarked on by Khrushchev was inaugurated in 1965. The essence of the scheme, as originally propounded, was to allow a considerable freedom of initiative to managers of enterprises who were to be encouraged to gear their products to the requirements of the consumer, rather than to the dictates of the plan, and to be rewarded by material incentives for their success in satisfying the consumers. This reform ran into diffi-culties from the start. It was virtually sabotaged by the party officials, who feared loss of their authority, and by the central planners, who were accustomed to a command economy and did not wish to change. (There was also opposition from some mana-gers who preferred the old system to which they had learned to accommodate themselves.) By 1969, if not before, as was dis-closed in a round-table discussion, it became evident that the degree of central interference in management of industry remained quite unaffected by the reform: the example of Czechoslovakia, which had clearly shown the close connexion between economic reform and loss of party control, no doubt contributed to the demise of this bold Soviet attempt at decentralisation.

The organisation of industry has remained ever since a problem to which no final solution has been found. Trends which are clearly discernible are the restoration of the authority of the Ministries at the top, and considerable increase in the authority and influence of the party organisations at enterprise level, after a short period during which their authority seemed to be declining. The powers of the party organisations within the Central Ministries have also been recently strengthened in the sense that they are now directly authorised to check on the fulfilment by the Ministry in which they operate of its duties. The 24th Congress of the CPSU in 1971, without specifically saying so, virtually acknowledged the demise of the 1965 reform by emphasis on the two factors which were henceforth to dominate industrial organisation: intensified supervision and direction by the party, and reliance on technology to improve production.

A different kind of attempt at decentralisation of industrial organisation was embarked on in April 1973. Direct ministerial control over enterprises was replaced by a system of delegated control by industrial combines, or unions. The idea behind the reform is that the combines (on which the managers of enterprises are represented but enjoy little power) should deal with most administrative matters, while the ministries deal with overall policy matters. It is too early to say to what extent this system has improved or altered the previous system of direct command. There is one indication that the old command system still prevails. An enormous Directors' Council—consisting of Director and Deputy Director of the Combine, managers of enterprises and representatives of the trade unions—has been interposed between the Director General of the Combine and individual enterprises in order, so the official version runs, to facilitate smooth relations between the Combine and the enterprises. It seems clear that so large a body cannot effectively take decisions, which will therefore fall to its Chairman who is empowered to decide where agreement cannot be reached—and he is the same as the Director General of the Combine. So it looks as if we are back at the command system after all.

There are at least two other, modern, factors in the Soviet system which operate to produce a high degree of centralisation.

One is the emphasis on technology, particularly since 1971. This has resulted in the development of a process already initiated by Khrushchev, namely the increasing attention to the technological training in the case of the higher party officials. Thus, to quote the most recent figures available, in 1952 only 18·4 per cent of city and district party secretaries were university educated; by 1973 the percentage was 97·7, and in the case of republican and regional party secretaries the figures were 67·7% and 99·2%. As of 1977, it is 99·4%. (University education of those who embark on a professional career in the party is almost invariably technical or scientific.) Since university education among rank and file members is very much the exception, especially since the growing attempt in recent years to increase the proportion of workers and peasants in the party, there is a tendency for the leading party officials to become a technical élite. This growth of an élite within the party is scarcely conducive to any encouragement of decentralisation, let alone democracy, within the party.

The other new factor which increases fears of decentralisation at the top is the growth in some of the Union Republics of economic nationalism—something comparable to the 'localism' among the regional secretaries which developed as the result of Khrushchev's economic re-organisation of 1957. This means the attempt by perfectly loyal Communist officials in some republics, who may not (consciously at any rate) have any trace of political nationalism in their temperament, to try to defend the economic interests and priorities in their republics against encroachment by the All Union economic policy—where the two kinds of interests compete. This, for example, is what happened in the Ukraine in the years preceding 1973 which witnessed the downfall and removal from the Politburo of the First Secretary of the Communist Party of the Ukraine, P. E. Shelest. Shortly before the Plenum of the Central Committee, which removed him from the Politburo, Shelest was accused in the Ukrainian party journal of what amounted to economic (and in his case, perhaps not only economic) nationalism. The case of Shelest is not unique.

Of course, the fact that the Soviet Government operates a vast, centralised command economy does not mean that the Politburo and the Council of Ministers legislate without any regard for the wishes and interests of those affected by their actions. On the contrary, there exists an extensive system of consultation which the party and the Government embark on regularly as part of the process of legislation and administration.

This process of consultation has by some students of Soviet government been interpreted as a sign of the emergence of pressure and interest groups in the Soviet Union—though the process of consultation is by no means new in the Soviet Union. It takes place, and has taken place in the past, at all kinds of levels and instances. There are conferences and consultations organised by the Central Committee, by the Ministries, by the Council of Ministers, by various Institutes, by the Supreme Soviet Commissions and by the apparatus of the Central Committee of the CPSU —to mention the main instances. However, there is a close connection between democratic government and the effectiveness of groups or persons who seek to influence a government: if there is no democracy, the effectiveness of such lobbying is very much reduced. Analysis of the operation of the process of consultation in the USSR shows that the following main limitations operate: (a) the absence of any kind of democratic control over the process of legislation that ultimately emerges after consultation means that the government can effectively ignore advice which it finds inconvenient or for any reason objectionable, without being called to account; (b) since the selection of delegates for consultation rests entirely with the government, the government can omit the independent-minded, the trouble shooters and the critics from their list; (c) there is a strong instinct among many, the majority probably, of Soviet citizens to let well alone so as not to disturb vested interests; (d) there is often a natural reluctance to speak one's mind too openly in the presence of the government for fear that this might have unpleasant consequences for one's career.

It is, to say the least, probable that the policy of *détente* with the United States on which the USSR embarked in 1972 was, at all events in part, connected with Soviet interest in US, and also in West European and Japanese, credits, technology and grain. All the evidence suggests that Soviet consumer production is seriously lagging behind in efficiency and in extent when compared with other major industrial powers. Attempts to introduce greater progress by the kind of decentralisation described above have foundered on political obstruction and on the vested interest of the Communist Party in retaining its overall control. The solution which the Soviet leaders have for some years past (certainly since the 24th Congress of the CPSU in 1971) envisaged lies in technology.

But technological development, so far as the consumer industry is concerned, founders on lack of capital for investment, and on the very high priority which the defence industry always claims in relation to available technology. Shortage of grain requirements also seems to be endemic in the Soviet system owing to a generally highly inefficient system of agriculture and the poverty of the soil in many areas. Soviet economic dependence on Western European and American credits and exports is illuminated by a few recent figures. Thus, in 1975 the Soviet Union imported more than four times as much machinery and equipment from the major non-Communist powers as in 1971—nearly four times as much from Japan, nearly seven times as much from West Germany and nearly twenty times as much from USA. Soviet indebtedness increased six- to eightfold (depending on the estimate one accepts), and it is planned to increase up to fifteen times the 1971 figure if necessary, according to a statement by the Soviet Prime Minister.

This economic motive for *détente* is not admitted by Soviet leaders, who prefer to advance as their motive the avoidance of conflict between the nuclear powers. That this cannot be the real motive, however, is evident from the fact that avoidance of nuclear conflict between the United States and the Soviet Union has been the policy of both these powers for many years before *détente* was spoken of. The cases of Cuba in 1962, of Vietnam after the large-scale Soviet military involvement had taken place after 1965, and the Middle Eastern conflict of 1967 are all cases in point. In all these instances direct negotiations between the two powers were embarked on (in some cases by means of the direct 'hot line' between Washington and Moscow) with the precise object of making sure that the two powers did not become involved in a nuclear conflict. It is reasonable to suppose (and much to be hoped) that, irrespective of the state of *détente*, such precautionary consultations will continue to take place in all future military crises. It is also probable that the Soviet Union may hope that the relations described as *détente* may lead to an agreement on curtailment of developments in the manufacture of weapons, in view of the high costs involved. But it is clear from the experience of the past few years that the Soviet Union will only contemplate agreement on the limitation of the production of armaments where it sees a distinct advantage to itself—as indeed may be supposed to be the American position as well. What is certain beyond any possible doubt is that *détente* does not, in Soviet interpretation, mean a relaxation of tension in international relations between the Communist and non-Communist parts of the world: on the contrary, the Soviet leaders have repeatedly asserted that *détente* does not mean the abandonment of ideological conflict between the two systems, but that it in fact entails a heightening of that conflict. Experience suggests that 'ideological conflict' is very widely interpreted to include for example, support for 'liberation movements' in Africa, or for a Communist revolution in Portugal.

One of the most remarkable developments of the past decade has been the rise of a dissent or dissident movement of protest in the USSR, which takes on a great variety of forms. Though there have existed some small conspiratorial opposition groups, the overwhelming majority of dissenters have no violent aims: in one form or another they assert rights which they contend are already enshrined in the laws of the Soviet Union. Their main weapon has been publicity. This has been achieved through the medium of what has become known the world over as *samizdat*: unofficially circulated documents, ranging from signed protests against particular abuses to entire symposia of articles, and books. This material has found its way abroad where it is published and made known outside the Soviet Union, but also finds its way back to the USSR by means of broadcasts, and in printed form. The most comprehensive publication has been the *Chronicle of Current Events*, a *samizdat* regular record, which has achieved a reputation for scrupulous accuracy, of judicial and extra-judicial persecution of individuals for their opinions, severe conditions in labour camps and mental hospitals in which some dissenters are confined, and the persecution of religious believers and minority nationalities. The *Chronicle* began to appear in 1968 every two months and has appeared regularly ever since with an interruption from the end of 1972 for over two years during which the Soviet security forces had succeeded in silencing it. Those responsible for producing the *Chronicle* remain anonymous, for obvious reasons of survival. But there exists a fairly numerous group of those who try to defend human rights who seek the maximum publicity for their protests against abuses and who use all means at their disposal to make them as widely known as possible in the Western world. This, the main group of dissenters, includes a wide variety: there are those whose protest is directed at violations of Soviet law against individuals and similar abuses; there are national groups such as the Jews, many of whom seek the right to emigrate, and Ukrainians and many other nationalities who protest about the suppression of their rights to use their language and pursue their cultural life. Then there are religious bodies, both orthodox and others such as the Baptists, who protest about the failure of the authorities to allow them even the restricted religious freedom permitted by law, or the Catholics of Lithuania who protest about the persecutions to which they are subjected. There are also groups and individuals whose dissenting views reflect varying degrees of Russian nationalism and traditionalism—ranging from those, often called 'neo-slavophiles' to those who hold more extreme views.

The reaction of the Soviet authorities has varied. There have been numerous trials, followed by severe sentences; many dissenters have been confined to mental hospitals and subjected there to appalling 'treatment'. In yet other cases prominent dissenters have either been allowed to emigrate, or, if unwilling (like Solzhenitsyn), forcibly deported. A report by Amnesty International, published in 1975, estimated the number of political prisoners in Soviet prisons and camps as 'at least 10,000', and this figure did not include those confined in the mental hospitals and prisons. Nevertheless, up to the present (March 1977) the Soviet authorities have not succeeded in stifling this movement. There has been a measure of success achieved by the protesters: well over 100,000 Jews have been allowed to emigrate, usually after harrassment, the *Chronicle* has re-appeared and the Western press carries regular accounts of the abuses and violations of law which the authorities perpetrate. The whole question of dissent raises several vital questions on Soviet politics: What is its significance? Why have the Soviet authorities not completely suppressed it? In what way, if any, does it modify Soviet policy?

Although one is dealing at most with a few thousand individuals in a population of 250 million their significance should not be minimised. Their voices have had the effect of ensuring that the Soviet Union is no longer the closed society that it has for so long sought to make itself, projecting the image of itself which it desired to project with as much disregard for truth in its propaganda as it thought necessary. This it can no longer do, or at any rate cannot do to the same extent as before. Why, then, has dissent not been even more vigorously repressed than it has? In part the answer may lie in the nature of the Soviet system of government as it has evolved since the death of Stalin. From a personal despotism it has become a collective leadership—to a greater or lesser degree at different times—but still a collective leadership in which one man, however influential, still has to ensure the support of his colleagues in order to rule. But terror on the scale which would be required in order to suppress dissent now is not so easily practised by a committee as it is by one all-powerful ruler. Those who would have to carry out the ruthless policy of suppression might well find their zeal dampened by the thought that the present leaders could be replaced by others, to whom they would have to answer for their actions—as Beria and many of his close associates paid the penalty when Stalin died. But a policy of all-out repression, though less easy now than under Stalin, is not impossible; only time will show whether or no it will be resorted to.

There is, however, another, new inhibiting factor on Soviet treatment of dissent: world public opinion. This should not be exaggerated. It did not in 1968 prevent Soviet invasion of Czechoslovakia in order to suppress a régime which had attempted to introduce some elements of democracy into Communist rule, in spite of the widespread criticism of the USSR which this action inevitably aroused. But the Soviet leaders have to look carefully at two areas in particular where their treatment of dissenters produces repercussions. One is the United States and the countries of Western Europe to which the USSR looks for economic bolstering. It is impossible for the Soviet leaders to ignore altogether the reaction of these countries to the treatment which they mete out to non-violent critics of their system. In terms of democratic government these men have committed no offence, and the Soviet Union cannot always entirely ignore the possibility that the resentment of the Western democracies at Soviet behaviour might have repercussions in terms of trade—or credits and technological aid in particular. The second area to which the Soviet leaders must look for reactions to their policy in respect of dissidents is that of the Western Communist parties who have recently, no doubt with their own electorates in mind, become severe critics of Soviet repressive policy. This question of the influence on Soviet policy of Western reaction is comparatively recent. It has been brought about by the growing knowledge of Soviet repressive methods, for the dissemination of which the dissidents are largely responsible—both those inside Russia and those who have emigrated or been expelled. It is too early at this date to make any confident prediction of the degree to which this new factor can be expected to bring about modifications in Soviet domestic policy either in the direction of greater repression or towards greater liberalisation.

There have been few major political developments in the past decade. The Politburo is still a collective leadership, even if the influence of the General Secretary has steadily increased, especially in the sphere of foreign policy which, theoretically, belongs to the area of competence of the Prime Minister. But the General Secretary cannot act as a dictator: he has to consult his colleagues and ensure that he can carry them with him. At present (1977), he appears to enjoy a safe majority support among his colleagues, especially since, in the last few years, several Politburo members who were believed to oppose him (such as Polyansky, Shelepin or Shelest) have been ousted.

The latest information on the composition of the CPSU, released in May 1976, revealed few significant changes. The over 15⅛ million members and candidates form 9·3 per cent of the adult population. The social position of members remains virtually unchanged. Over 44 per cent are described as 'employees', and this figure does not include the numerous, probably the majority, of those described as peasants and workers who are in fact in white-collar posts. The percentage of women has increased to nearly 30, and nearly one-quarter of members have completed higher education. Among secretaries of regional district and city party committees—in other words, in the party apparatus—the percentage of those with higher education is (as already noted) over 99. Since in the great majority of cases this means technical or scientific education, it is evident that the growth of a technical élite among the party professionals (which was referred to above) is still proceeding.

No recent information has been published on the age of party members, but all indications are that the great majority are young. For example, according to official statistics 67·2 per cent of all party members have been members for between five and twenty years, which suggests that their age is between thirty and forty-five. Over three-quarters of all party members have joined since the war and one-third only became Communists in the last ten years. This means, in effect, that over two-thirds of all party members have joined since the death of Stalin in 1953 and are, as it were, 'untainted' by the conditions which prevailed during his period of rule. A very different picture emerges if we look at those in leading positions in the party apparatus. In the Politburo, for example, the average age is approaching seventy, and only very few members are under fifty. Similarly, while exact figures for the present position are not available, it is safe to assume that only a small proportion of regional first secretaries—the key men of the party apparatus, who are on the promotion ladder for highest party office—is younger than fifty.

There is therefore a substantial age gap between party leaders and party rank and file. This fact has naturally prompted speculation about the kind of changes, if any, which can be expected when in due course the turn comes for the younger men to take over the leadership of the country. Two diametrically opposed arguments can be advanced. On the one hand, it can be convincingly contended that these younger men, and especially those who have joined the party since the death of Stalin, have made their careers in a more relaxed atmosphere, with greater opportunities than those enjoyed by their elders for making contacts outside the USSR, and with some knowledge of the world beyond the narrow horizons of the Communist-controlled block. Therefore, it is said, when their time comes to rule they can be expected to be more flexible, less dogmatic, less ideologically limited than their elders. The opposite case is that the younger men have experienced the horrors of neither the war nor of Stalin's régime of terror. Therefore they cannot be expected to exercise the restraint which the fear of the repetition of those terrible years induces in those who are senior to them, who know only too well what war means and who have felt their own necks at risk while Stalin was at the helm. Therefore, it is said the younger men, when their turn at the top comes round, will be more ruthless, more determined, more uncompromising than those whom they succeed. The reader must make his or her own choice between these two conjectures.

On 7 October 1977 the Supreme Soviet in an extraordinary joint session of both chambers adopted a new Constitution with immediate effect by a unanimous vote. The 7 October was declared henceforth an annual public holiday. Some time before this session the General Secretary of the CPSU was elected Chairman of the Praesidium of the Supreme Soviet. This combination of offices, while new in Soviet practice, is found in some of the

'People's Republics'. It is not inconsistent either with the 1936 or the 1977 Constitution.

The new Constitution is longer than the old—174 Articles as against 146. Even though, as will be seen, the changes of substance are few, the document has been completely re-written from beginning to end. If the Constitution were subject to any form of review in the courts, these numerous changes of language would entail years of litigation. But since there is no form of judicial review embodied in the new Constitution, any more than in the old, and since in practice constitutional issues cannot be raised in the courts by Soviet litigants, no problems of interpretation will arise in this form.

The new Constitution has made virtually no changes in the structure of the Soviet state. It is, as before, federal, in form: Article 73, which replaces Article 14 of the 1936 Constitution, though somewhat more compact than its predecessor, confers all the same powers as before on the All-Union government. The Union Republics are granted, as before, the, somewhat academic, right freely to secede from the Union (Article 72). However, the rights of the Union Republics are more fully specified in Articles 76 to 81 than they were in old articles 15 to 18, and the Union government is specifically enjoined (in Article 81) to safeguard the sovereign powers of the Union Republics. The provisions for the functioning of the Supreme Soviet, its two Chambers and its Praesidium, now covered by Articles 108–127, are substantially as set out in Articles 30–56 of the 1936 Constitution. There are some minor changes. For example, 32 deputies are now to be elected for each Union Republic instead of 25 (Article 110); and two new items are enumerated under the powers of the Praesidium of the Supreme Soviet: the setting up of the Defence Council, the supreme military policy-making body of which the existence has only very recently been revealed (Article 121 (14)); and 'checking on the observance of the Constitution of the USSR' (Article 121 (4)). The new provisions for the Council of Ministers (Articles 128–136) are somewhat more detailed than the former Article, but introduce little which is substantially new. There is one innovation—presumably on grounds of convenience. Article 70 of the 1936 Constitution specified the long list of individual ministers and ministries. Since this required frequent alteration between sessions of the Supreme Soviet, it used to be a regular feature of each session for an amendment of Article 70 to be adopted—with all the formalities which this entailed: these details will now be dealt with on the basis of a separate statute (Article 136).

No changes of substance have been introduced in the articles dealing with the electoral system (Articles 95–102) or the court (Articles 151–163), though the provisions of the latter are more detailed and more declamatory on the rights of the accused than Articles 102–112 of the 1936 Constitution. The rights specified (such as equality before the law, or that no one can be sentenced except in a court of law) are already enacted in the relevant criminal codes: whether their enshrining in the Constitution will make any difference in practice remains to be seen. There is one substantial change in the provision for the appointment of the Procurator General: this is now to be for five years (Article 167), and not as hitherto seven years (Article 114 of the 1936 Constitution). Nothing is said about the practice of re-appointing the Procurator General on the expiry of his term, which has been the case with the present incumbent.

The main innovations of 1977 are to be found in the Preamble and in the declamatory parts of the Constitution, and in the provisions relating to the rights and duties of citizens. Three points are of particular interest. Article 1 describes the USSR as an 'all peoples' state'. This is the formulation that was already adopted in the Party Programme of 1961 and signifies the abandonment of the notion of the dictatorship of the proletariat and of class conflict. Secondly, there is specific mention (in the Preamble) of the 'international position of the USSR as an integral part of the world socialist system'. Article 28, after reciting constant Soviet striving for peace and international co-operation, apparently incorporates the so-called 'Brezhnev Doctrine' on the right of one socialist country to intervene in the defence of socialism in another country if it should be threatened: the article includes in its recital of the international policy of the Soviet Union 'the strengthening of the position of world socialism'. Thirdly, Article 6 describes the Communist Party as the 'guiding and directing force of Soviet society, the core of its political system and of state and public organisations'. This has, of course, been the case in practice since 1917. But it is the first time that a constitution has described the reality so directly. The Constitutions of 1918 and 1924 made no mention whatever of the Communist Party. The Constitution of 1936, in Article 126 which dealt with the right of citizens to unite in public organisations, mentioned the Communist Party as the organisation favoured by the most active and most conscious citizens, and went on to describe it as the 'leading core' of the public and state organisations.

The chapter on 'Fundamental Rights, Freedoms and Duties of the Citizen of the USSR', Ch. VII, embodying Articles 39 to 69, is longer and more verbose than Chapter 10 of the 1936 Constitution, which contained sixteen articles. Although this chapter embodies some new rights, it re-enacts the old limitation and introduces a new one. The old limitation is that the basic rights of free speech and press are granted 'in accordance with the interests of the people and with the aim of strengthening and developing the socialist system'. In the absence of any provision for judicial interpretation of this phrase, the situation will remain as before: the Communist Party will determine these limits. The new restriction is contained in Article 39: enjoyment of the rights conferred by the Constitution 'must not harm the interests of society and the state or the rights of other citizens'. Again, in the absence of judicial review, the decision on what is harmful to society and the state will rest with the party or the security organs, and experience has shown how arbitrary these can be.

Apart from extensive guarantees of the right to enjoy the cultural heritage and free scientific and artistic creativity (again 'in accordance with the aims of constructing communism') there is an innovation which may prove of some significance. Article 58 confers the right of 'complaint' against state and public organs—which presumably includes, in theory, the Communist Party. But, what is more interesting, is the new right conferred of bringing action in the courts against officials who act unlawfully or in excess of their powers. There is also a right to recover compensation for unlawful acts by state and public organisations and by officials—though it is not, in this instance, stated that compensation can be sought in the courts. The effect of these provisions remains to be seen. If the courts are really allowed to deal with unlawful acts by officials and organisations, and if the courts behave with greater impartiality than they have in the past when dealing with conflicts between citizen and state, the results could be far-reaching. It is too early (June 1978) to be excessively optimistic.

APPENDIX

THE COUNCIL OF MINISTERS OF THE USSR
as at 15 December 1976

Chairman

First Deputy Chairmen (2)

Deputy Chairmen (10)
including Chairman, State Planning Committee (Gosplan) (UR)
Chairman, State Committee for Science and Technology (AU)
Chairman, State Committee for Construction Affairs (Gosstroi) (UR)
Chairman, State Committee for Material-Technical Supply (UR)

Ministries (61)

All-Union (31) (A-U: i.e. there are no corresponding Ministries in the
Republics)
Automobile industry
Aviation industry
Chemical industry
Chemical and oil machine building
Civil aviation
Communications equipment industry
Construction, road and municipal machine building
Defence industry
Electronics industry
Electrical engineering industry
Foreign trade
Gas industry
General machine building
Heavy and transport machine building
Instrument-making, means of automation and control systems
Machine building
Machine building for light and food industry and domestic appliances

Machine building for livestock farming and animal foods production
Machine-tool building and tool industry
Medical industry
Medium machine building
Merchant marine
Oil industry
Petroleum and gas industry enterprises construction
Power machine building
Pulp and paper industry
Radio industry
Ship building industry
Tractor and agricultural machine building
Transport
Transport construction

Union Republic (31) (UR: i.e. there are corresponding Ministries or
    Committees in the Republics)
Agricultural procurement
Agriculture
Coal industry
Communications
Construction
Construction of heavy industry enterprises
Construction (industrial)
Construction (rural)
Construction—materials industry
Culture
Defence
Education
Erection and special construction work
Ferrous metallurgy
Finance
Fisheries
Food industry
Foreign affairs
Geology
Health
Higher and secondary specialised education
Internal affairs
Justice
Land reclamation and water economy
Light industry
Meat and milk industry
Non-ferrous metallurgy
Oil-processing and petro-chemical industry
Power and electrification
Timber and wood processing industry
Trade

State Committees of the Council of Ministers (10)
Foreign economic relations
Forestry
Inventions and discoveries
Labour and social questions (UR) (changed August 1976)
Prices
Professional and technical education
Television and broadcasting
Standards
Cinematography
Publishing, polygraphy and the book trade

Other members of the Council of Ministers, USSR
Chairman, Board of State Bank
Head, Central Statistical Administration
Chairman, 'Soyuzselkhoztekhnika' (Agricultural Machinery Corporation)
Chairman, Committee of People's Control
Chairman, Committee for State Security

Chairmen of Republic Councils of Ministers (15)
Armenia
Azerbaidzhan
Belorussia
Estonia
Georgia
Kazakhstan
Kirgizia
Latvia
Lithuania
Moldavia
RSFSR
Tadzhikistan
Turkmenistan
Ukraine
Uzbekistan

Committees 'attached to' the Council of Ministers
TASS
Physical Culture and Sport
Supervision of Safety in Industry and Mining

Other Committees
Civil Construction and Architecture (under Gosstroi)
Use of Atomic Energy (of the USSR)

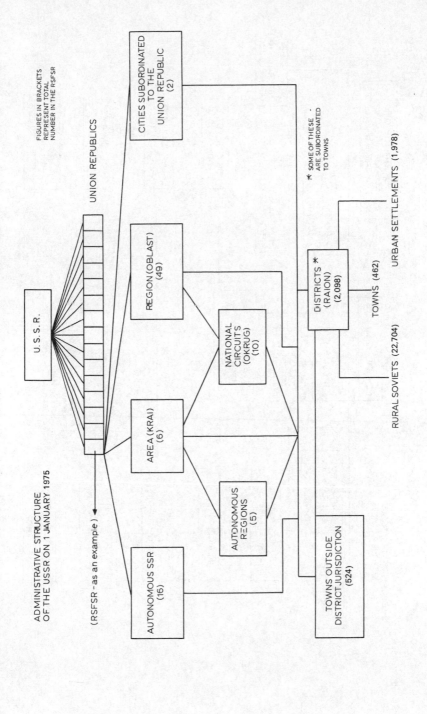

ADMINISTRATIVE STRUCTURE
OF THE USSR ON 1 JANUARY 1975

FIGURES IN BRACKETS
REPRESENT TOTAL
NUMBER IN THE RSFSR

(RSFSR - as an example)

U. S. S. R.

UNION REPUBLICS

CITIES SUBORDINATED
TO THE
UNION REPUBLIC
(2)

AUTONOMOUS SSR
(16)

AREA (KRAI)
(6)

REGION (OBLAST)
(49)

NATIONAL
CIRCUITS
(OKRUG)
(10)

AUTONOMOUS
REGIONS
(5)

* SOME OF THESE -
ARE SUBORDINATED
TO TOWNS

DISTRICTS *
(RAION)
(2,098)

TOWNS OUTSIDE
DISTRICT JURISDICTION
(524)

URBAN SETTLEMENTS (1,978)

TOWNS (462)

RURAL SOVIETS (22,704)

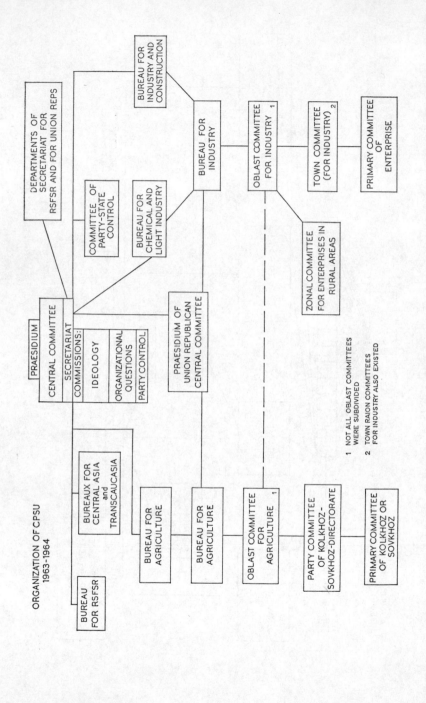

ORGANIZATION OF CPSU
1963-1964

PRAESIDIUM

CENTRAL COMMITTEE

SECRETARIAT

COMMISSIONS:
IDEOLOGY
ORGANIZATIONAL QUESTIONS
PARTY CONTROL

DEPARTMENTS OF SECRETARIAT FOR RSFSR AND FOR UNION REPS

BUREAU FOR INDUSTRY AND CONSTRUCTION

COMMITTEE OF PARTY-STATE CONTROL

BUREAU FOR CHEMICAL AND LIGHT INDUSTRY

BUREAU FOR INDUSTRY

OBLAST COMMITTEE FOR INDUSTRY [1]

TOWN COMMITTEE (FOR INDUSTRY) [2]

PRIMARY COMMITTEE OF ENTERPRISE

ZONAL COMMITTEE FOR ENTERPRISES IN RURAL AREAS

PRAESIDIUM OF UNION REPUBLICAN CENTRAL COMMITTEE

BUREAU FOR RSFSR

BUREAUX FOR CENTRAL ASIA and TRANSCAUCASIA

BUREAU FOR AGRICULTURE

BUREAU FOR AGRICULTURE

OBLAST COMMITTEE FOR AGRICULTURE [1]

PARTY COMMITTEE OF KOLKHOZ-SOVKHOZ-DIRECTORATE

PRIMARY COMMITTEE OF KOLKHOZ OR SOVKHOZ

1 NOT ALL OBLAST COMMITTEES WERE SUBDIVIDED

2 TOWN RAION COMMITTEES FOR INDUSTRY ALSO EXISTED

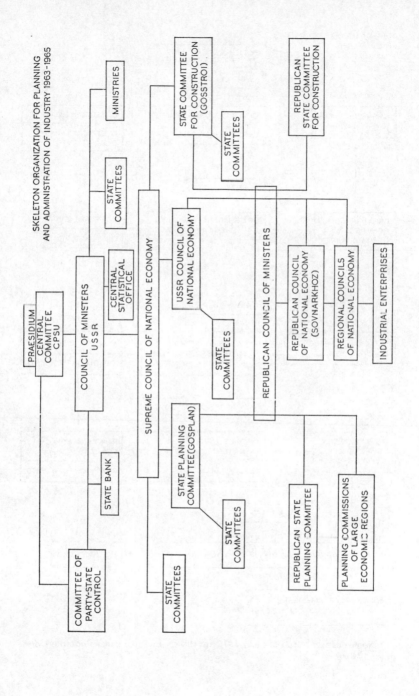

SKELETON ORGANIZATION FOR PLANNING
AND ADMINISTRATION OF INDUSTRY 1963-1965

PRAESIDIUM
CENTRAL
COMMITTEE
CPSU

COMMITTEE OF PARTY-STATE CONTROL

COUNCIL OF MINISTERS USSR

STATE BANK

CENTRAL STATISTICAL OFFICE

STATE COMMITTEES

MINISTRIES

STATE COMMITTEE FOR CONSTRUCTION (GOSSTROI)

STATE COMMITTEES

REPUBLICAN STATE COMMITTEE FOR CONSTRUCTION

SUPREME COUNCIL OF NATIONAL ECONOMY

USSR COUNCIL OF NATIONAL ECONOMY

STATE COMMITTEES

STATE PLANNING COMMITTEE (GOSPLAN)

STATE COMMITTEES

REPUBLICAN COUNCIL OF MINISTERS

REPUBLICAN COUNCIL OF NATIONAL ECONOMY (SOVNARKHOZ)

REGIONAL COUNCILS OF NATIONAL ECONOMY

INDUSTRIAL ENTERPRISES

REPUBLICAN STATE PLANNING COMMITTEE

PLANNING COMMISSIONS OF LARGE ECONOMIC REGIONS

ORGANISATION OF THE CPSU
February 1976*

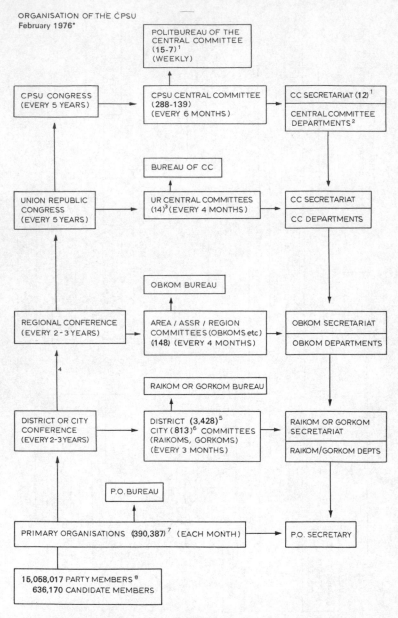

* Some changes since February 1976 are shown on Table under Footnote 1 on pages 179–80.

I *The interlocking Party and Government leadership* of the USSR as at 15 December 1976 was as follows:

Politburo CPSU	Secretariat CPSU	Council of Ministers	Other functions
Full Members (15)			
Brezhnev, L. I. 70 (1957)	Brezhnev, L. I. Secretary-General (1964)		Member, Presidium, Supreme Soviet USSR (1965)
Andropov, Yu. V. 62 (1973)		Andropov, Yu. V. Chairman Committee for State Security (1967)	
Grishin, V. V. 62 (1971)			1st Secretary, Moscow *Gorkom* (1967); Member, Presidium, Supreme Soviet USSR (1967)
Gromyko, A. A. 67 (1973)		Gromyko, A. A. Minister of Foreign Affairs (1957)	
Kirilenko, A. P. 70 (1962)	Kirilenko, A. P. (1966)		
Kosygin, A. N. 72 (1960)		Kosygin, A. N. Chairman (1964	
Kulakov, F. D. 58 (1971)	Kulakov, F. D. (1965)		Head, Agriculture Department, CC, CPSU (1964) until May 1976
Kunaev, D. A. 64 (1971)			1st Secretary, CC, Kazakhstan (1964); Member, Presidium, Supreme Soviet USSR (1962)
Mazurov, K. T. 62 (1965)		Mazurov, K. T. 1st Deputy Chairman (1965)	
Pelshe, A. Ya. 77 (1966)			Chairman, Party Control Committee (1966)
Podgorny, N. V. 73 (1960)			President, Presidium, Supreme Soviet USSR, (1965)
Romanov, G. V. 53 (March 1976)			1st Secretary, Leningrad *Obkom* (1970) Member Presidium Supreme Soviet USSR (Nov. 1971)

Note
Figures outside brackets indicate age at 1 January 1977. Figures in brackets indicate year from which position has been held continuously.

Politburo CPSU	*Secretariat* CPSU	*Council of Ministers*	*Other functions*
Full Members			
Shcherbitsky, V. V. 58 (1971)			1st Secretary, CC, Ukraine, (1972) Member, Presidium, Supreme Soviet USSR, (1972)
Suslov, M. A. 74 (1955)	Suslov, M. A. (1947)		Chairman, Foreign Affairs Commission, Council of the Union (1954)
Ustinov, D. F. 68 (1976 March)	Ustinov, D. F. (1965)	Minister of Defence (April 1976)	
Candidate Members (7)			
Aliev, G. A. 53 (March 1976)			1st Secretary, CC, Azerbeidzhan (1969)
Demichev, P. N. 58 (1964)		Minister of Culture (1974)	
Masherov, P. M. 58 (1966)			1st Secretary, CC, Belorussia (1965) Member, Presidium, Supreme Soviet USSR, (1966)
Ponomarev, B. N. 71 (1972)	Ponomarev, B. N. (1961)		Head, International Department, CC, CPSU (1955); Chairman, Foreign Affairs Commission, Council of Nationalities (1964)
Rashidov, Sh. R. 59 (1961)			1st Secretary, CC, Uzbekistan (1959) Member, Presidium, Supreme Soviet USSR, (1970)
Solomentsev, M. S. 63 (1971)			Chairman, Council of Ministers, RSFSR (1971)
	Dolgikh, V. I. 52 (1972)		
	Kapitonov, I. V. 61 (1965)		Head, Department for Organisational Party Work, CC, CPSU (1965)
	Katushev, K. F. 49 (1968)		
	Zimyanin, M. V. 62 (March 1976)		Deputy Chairman Foreign Affairs Commission, Council of Nationalities (1974)
			Chernenko, K. U.
	Chernenko, K. U. 65 (March 1976)		Head General Department CC, CPSU (1965)
	Ryabov, Ya. P. 48 (Oct 1976)		Chairman, Industry Commission, Council of Union (1974)

2 A list of the CC Departments (administered by the CC Secretariat) is never published, but the situation as known in January 1977 was roughly as follows:

Administration of Affairs (G. S. Pavlov)
Administrative Organs (N. I. Savinkin)
Agriculture (presumably F. D. Kulakov)
Chemical Industry (V. M. Bushuev)
Construction (I. N. Dmitriev)
Cultural Department (V. F. Shauro)
Defence Industry (I. D. Serbin)
General (K. U. Chernenko)
Heavy Industry (presumably V. I. Dolgikh)
International (B. N. Ponomarev)
Light and Food Industry (P. K. Sizov)
Machine Building (V. S. Frolov)
Organisational-Party Work (I. V. Kapitonov)
Personnel Abroad (A. S. Panyushkin)
Planning and Financial Organs (not known)
Propaganda (presumably P. N. Demichev)
Relations with Communist and Workers' Parties of Socialist Republics (presumably K. F. Katushev)
Science and Educational Establishments (S. P. Trapeznikov)
Trade and Public Services (Ya. I. Kabkov)
Transport and Communications (K. S. Simonov)
Party Control Committee (A. Ya. Pel'she)
Chief Political Directorate of the Army and Navy (A. A. Epishev)

3 N.B. The RSFSR has no Party organisation of its own.

4 A minor tier has been omitted here for simplicity: the 10 National Circuits (okrugs) in the RSFSR have their own Party committees and thus form an extra tier in the hierarchy.

5 This figure is for 1 January 1976. It includes 2,857 rural district committees, 571 urban district committees (subordinate to city committees). A number of miscellaneous committees (merchant navy, etc.) also have the status of district committees.

6 Figure for 1 January 1976. N.B. Some city committees are directly subordinate to the CC's of Union Republics.

7 Figure for 1 January 1976.

8 Figure for February 1976 (number represented at 24th Congress).

Chart prepared by P. B. Reddaway and updated by Miss Xenia Howard-Johnston, and reproduced here by their kind permission.

SUGGESTIONS FOR FURTHER READING

The literature on the history and institutions of the Soviet Union is vast, and only a very few titles which are likely to be helpful for more detailed study are included here. A comprehensive bibliography will be found in Fainsod, *How Russia is Ruled*.

1 HISTORICAL BACKGROUND

R. Charques, *The Twilight of Imperial Russia*, 1959
(A short but valuable study of the last reign of Imperial Russia)

M. Florinsky, *Russia: A History and Interpretation*, Vol. II, 1953
(One of the most complete and informative histories in English of Russia from the reign of Alexander I till the Revolution of 1917)

G. H. N. Seton-Watson, *The Russian Empire, 1801–1917*, 1967
(A valuable and authoritative survey of all aspects of Russian history, including institutions, from Alexander I to 1917)

J. Walkin, *The Rise of Democracy in Pre-Revolutionary Russia*, 1962
(An excellent study of the social background to the revolution)

2 HISTORY OF THE SOVIET PERIOD

E. H. Carr, *A History of Soviet Russia*, 9 volumes, 1950–
(An immensely detailed study, which although critical in its treatment tends to give more of a picture of official policy than of the history of the country)

W. H. Chamberlin, *The Russian Revolution*, 1935
(Although published thirty years ago, this is still a valuable history of the February and October Revolutions and the civil war)

The History of the Communist Party of the Soviet Union, second edition, 1962
(The second version to date of the official history published since Stalin's death. Totally unreliable on facts, but gives a good idea of the latest officially approved version of the facts)

G. Katkov, *Russia 1917: the February Revolution*, 1967
(Essential reading on the collapse of the Monarchy)

A. Nove, *An Economic History of the USSR*, 1969
(The best short economic history of the period)

R. Pipes, *The Formation of the Soviet Union*, second edition, 1964
(An authoritative study of the origins and development of Soviet national policy up to 1923)

L. Schapiro, *The Origin of the Communist Autocracy*, second edition, 1976 (A study of the socialist opponents of the Bolsheviks between 1917 and 1922)

3 MARXISM AND LENINISM

Shlomo Avineri, *The Social and Political Thought of Karl Marx*, 1968
(The best analytical study of the subject)

The Communist Manifesto, 1848

The Foundations of Marxism-Leninism, 1963 edition
(The officially sponsored Soviet textbook of ideology)

V. I. Lenin, *What is to be Done*, 1902
           State and Revolution, 1918
(The basic texts of Leninism)

G. Lichtheim, *Marxism*, 1961 (revised, 1964)
(An illuminating study of Marxism in its historical perspective)

R. N. Carew Hunt, *The Theory and Practice of Communism*, 1963
(Penguin edition)
(A critical, but impartial and fair, analysis of the ideas of Marx and Lenin. Contains a useful bibliography)

4 POLITICAL, LEGAL AND ECONOMIC INSTITUTIONS

The Soviet Constitution, 1936, as amended to date

The Rules of the CPSU, 1961

J. Armstrong, *The Politics of Totalitarianism: The CPSU from 1934 to the Present*, 1961
(A detailed study of Stalin's rule)

R. Auty and D. Obolensky (eds.), *Companion to Russian Studies*, volume 1, 1976
(A symposium of chapters on Russian and Soviet history and geography, and on Soviet political and economic structure)

F. Barghoorn, *Politics in the USSR*, 1966 (Written from the sociological angle)

M. Fainsod, *How Russia is Ruled*, second edition, 1963
(The most comprehensive, balanced and illuminating study of Soviet institutions in their historical and ideological setting. Quite indispensable to any serious student of the subject)

M. Fainsod, *Smolensk Under Soviet Rule*, 1958
(An analysis and summary, with ample quotations, of the records of the Smolensk Communist Party organisation from 1917 to 1941, which fell into British and US hands during the war. Throws a flood of authentic light on the practical operation of the Soviet system)

J. Hazard, *Law and Social Change in the USSR*, 1953
(A useful introduction to the function of law in Soviet society)

I. Lapenna, *Soviet Penal Policy*, 1968
(An excellent, clear summary of Soviet Criminal Law and Procedure)

A. Nove, *The Soviet Economy—An Introduction*, third edition, 1968,
(A clear and concise study of both the economic system and of the institutions through which it is maintained)

Peter Reddaway (Ed.), *Uncensored Russia*, 1972
(An important compendium of political information which has emerged in defiance of official censorship)

T. H. Rigby, *Communist Party Membership in the USSR: 1917–67* 1969
(The only complete study of the subject based on immense research)

L. Schapiro, *The Communist Party of the Soviet Union*, second edition, 1970
(A detailed study of the party from its origins until 1966)

D. J. R. Scott, *Russian Political Institutions*, fourth edition, 1969
(A concise yet detailed handbook of the political and administrative machinery)

G. H. N. Seton-Watson, *The Pattern of Communist Revolution*, second edition, 1960
(The standard work on the origins and development of the Communist system of rule. Published in USA under the title *From Lenin to Khrushchev*)

M. Tatu, *Power in the Kremlin*, 1969
(A good account of Khrushchev's period of rule and of his fall from power)

INDEX

Bold figures indicate main references

ACTIVISTS, 69, 108, 141–3, 153–4
Administrative personnel, 126–31, 149
Agricultural production administrations, *see* Kolkhoz-sovkhoz production directorates
Agriculture:
— collectivisation, **49–50**, 54, 76, 80, 99
— committees, 125
— land reform, 30, 32–3, 43, 47
— organisation, **125–6**, 141–2, 165
Akselrod, Pavel Borisovich (1850–1928), 16, 21–3, 29
Alexander II (1818–81; ruled from 1855), 17–18
All-Russian Communist Party (Bolsheviks), *see* Communist Party of the Soviet Union
All-Russian Social Democratic Labour Party, *see* Communist Party of the Soviet Union
All-Union Communist Party (Bolsheviks), *see* Communist Party of the Soviet Union
All-Union Leninist Communist League of Youth (Komsomol), **69–70,** 103, 143, 153
Amnesty International, 167
Anarchism, 17
'Anti-party group', 53, 72, 119
Areas, 63, 74, **98–102,** 136, 140, 153, 156

Armed forces, 38, 40, 51, 64, 66, 69, 83–4, 97, 112–13, 134, *see also* Law courts: Military courts
Armenia, 46, 82, *see also* Transcaucasia
Autonomous regions, 63, 74, 83, **98,** 102, 105, 110, 132–7
Autonomous republics, 63, 74, 83, 88, **97–8,** 102, 105, 110–11, 132–7, 150, 156
Azerbaijan, 46, 82, 96, 98, 132, *see also* Transcaucasia

BAKUNIN, Mikhail Aleksandrovich (1814–76), 17
Baltic States, 45–6, 96, 121, *see also* Estonia, Latvia, Lithuania
Belorussia, 46, 67, 82–3, 95–8, 101
Beria, Lavrentiy Pavlovich (1899–1953), 147, 168
Bernstein, Eduard (1850–1932), 21–2
Bloody Sunday (9/22 January 1905), 24
Bolsheviks, Ch. 1–2 *passim*
Border Guards, *see* State security service: Border Guards
Brezhnev, Leonid Ilyich (1906–), 54–5, 172
Budget, 84–5, 113–15, 135–41
Bukharin, Nikolay Ivanovich (1888–1938), 37, 41, 48–9, 80
Bulganin, Nikolay Aleksandrovich (1895–   ), 117